PHYLLIS TICKLE

EVANGELIST
OF
THE
FUTURE

PHYLLIS TICKLE

EVANGELIST OF THE FUTURE

Reflections on the Impact She's Had on Publishing, Religion, and the Church in America

EDITED AND WITH AN INTRODUCTION BY Tony Jones

PARACLETE PRESS
BREWSTER, MASSACHUSETTS

2014 First Printing

Phyllis Tickle: Evangelist of the Future

Copyright © 2014 by: Introduction, Tony Jones; Chapter One, Jon M. Sweeney; Chapter Two, Jana Riess; Chapter Three, Sister Danielle Dwyer; Chapter Four, Stephanie Spellers; Chapter Five, Ryan K. Bolger; Chapter Six, Brian D. McLaren; Chapter Seven, Sybil MacBeth; Chapter Eight, Doug Pagitt; Chapter Nine, Lauren F. Winner; Afterword, Diana Butler Bass; Annotated Bibliography, Kelly Pigott.

ISBN 978-1-61261-375-8

Library of Congress Cataloging-in-Publication Data is available.

10 9 8 7 6 5 4 3 2 1

Published by Paraclete Press
Brewster, Massachusetts
www.paracletepress.com

Printed in the United States of America

CONTENTS

PART II

PHYLLIS'S CHALLENGES TO MAINLINE, EVANGELICAL, AND EMERGENCE CHRISTIANS

PART III
PHYLLIS'S LEGACY AS MIDWIFE, FRIEND, AND PRAY-ER

INTRODUCTION

Tony Jones

When asked, "What does your husband do?" my wife, Courtney, replies, "He's a freelance theologian." She likes that response because (1) it usually gets a chuckle and (2) it doesn't make me sound like a pastor or professor who can't find work.

Truth be told, I love the freelance life. But it's not without anxiety. Yes, I get to write books, speak, teach, and take part-time work here and there, but I've also got to worry about things like health insurance and retirement without anyone to back me up.

I have taken more lessons on this way of life from Phyllis Tickle than from anyone else. She is the queen of freelance theologians. In fact, it'd be more accurate to call her an ecclesial gadfly. She shows up everywhere, and she's got an opinion on everything. I've seen Phyllis Tickle challenge a nave full of becollared Episcopal clergy to get their heads out of the sand, and I've seen her address a stadium of 10,000 evangelical youth pastors. At the latter, she made one guy so angry that he rushed the stage and looked like he was going to deck her. One of the conference organizers jumped in between them and restrained the ornery youth pastor.

And, like a superhero, Phyllis escaped into the night.

■ ■ ■

Festschrift is a bit of a strange word. As you might guess, it comes from German and means "a celebratory piece of writing." It's what the colleagues of a prominent theologian write when he or she retires. In academia, it's an honor both to have a Festschrift devoted to your work and to be asked to edit a Festschrift for one of your mentors.

But as a freelance academic—as one who travels the country and teaches clergy and laity outside the confines of a seminary faculty position—Phyllis doesn't have academic colleagues, per se. She's done more to teach church history, biblical interpretation, and practical theology than a truckload full of seminary professors, but without a faculty job, she wasn't going to get a Festschrift. That's why I approached Paraclete Press about this volume. Happily, they concurred: Phyllis deserves a Festschrift.

▪ ▪ ▪

Another thing that Phyllis and I have in common is a great love of the Latin language, so I'm quite sure that she will agree with me that the Latin term for this kind of volume is superior: *liber amicorum*—literally, "a book of friends."

This is, indeed, a collection of essays by Phyllis's friends. And, as much as I implored them to focus on Phyllis's *work*, on her *contribution to scholarship and church history*, and on her *challenges to future generations*, they continued to default to at least some mention of her as a person. What you will find in the pages that follow is a wonderful mix of the personal and the professional, from Sybil MacBeth telling about how Phyllis is her literary midwife to Jon M. Sweeney tracing the influential arc of Phyllis's work in the publishing industry. In each chapter, you'll get some of Phyllis the person and some of Phyllis the professional; some chapters lean more to one side, some to the other.

The plain fact is that you can't really reflect on Phyllis's work without reflecting on her as a person. If she likes you, she'll take you into her heart faster than a redneck superchicken. She did with me. If she doesn't like you, look out. (But chances are she'll like you.)

Here's the thing, Phyllis has a keen bullshitometer. She's shoveled her share of literal BS on her farm, and she's seen plenty of it in the church and publishing worlds. She can smell it from a mile away. And she doesn't like it. Recently, during an interview, National Public Radio's Krista Tippett jokingly told Phyllis that she's not very politically correct, and I've got to say that's one of the things that I love most about Phyllis. Maybe it's her age, or her Southern charm, or a combination thereof, but she's able to write and say things that would get the rest of us in a lot of hot water.

Phyllis gets in her own hot water from time to time. There was the aforementioned evangelical youth pastor who took exception to her talk. And there was the time when, on her home turf at St. Mary's Cathedral in Memphis, she suggested the birth control pill had allowed women to go back to work and thus stunted the spiritual development of a generation of children. Needless to say, that didn't go over very well with the feminists in the crowd, and the blogosphere expressed its displeasure for days afterward. I was shaken, since I'd organized the event along with Doug Pagitt.

I called Phyllis to see how she was doing with all of the criticism. She was completely unfazed.

■ ■ ■

Phyllis Natalie Alexander was born on March 12, 1934, to Philip Wade Alexander and Katherine Ann Porter Alexander. As Phyllis tells it, one Samuel Milton Tickle was in the next crib in the nursery at First Presbyterian Church of Johnson City, Tennessee— she was two weeks old, and he was exactly fifty weeks older than she. (He'll show up later in the story, as you might guess.)

Phyllis's dad was the dean of East Tennessee State University. Mom was a tennis fanatic and basketball coach, and during World War II, she taught in high school and college, though she lacked a college degree. Basically, she was the dean's wife—Mrs. Alexander's tea was a command performance every year, for the university faculty and for young Phyllis.

Phyllis spent her childhood in Johnson City at the university. Her first five years of life were spent in the men's dormitory, where her dad was not only dean but resident director. He decided young Phyllis was getting a bit used to the attention of 250 men, and so they bought a house off campus.

For her elementary, middle, and high school education, she attended the university's "Training School"—named such because it was staffed by teachers-in-training—and among her memories is that she was the only girl in physics class. As a student, Phyllis fell in love with Latin and Spanish and the way that human beings learn language.

At seventeen, Phyllis enrolled in Shorter College in Rome, Georgia. She flourished there, loved her teachers, and was instructed by some very powerful and influential women. Meanwhile, Sam—remember Sam?—was premed at East Tennessee State. For her senior year, she transferred to State because that's what dad wanted, and that's what Sam wanted, and Phyllis wanted to be with Sam. She graduated in March 1955, and started teaching Latin in Memphis public schools that September.

On June 17, 1955, Phyllis and Sam were married. In 1959, after Sam's internship, they moved to Pelzer, South Carolina, a small milling town. He was a country doctor there, and Phyllis worked as the business administrator of the hospital. They already had two kids and another on the way. In the early 1960s, Phyllis earned a master's degree at Furman University, was made a fellow of the university, and started teaching human growth and development there.

After a few years as a country doctor, Sam returned to training, specializing in pulmonology. By the mid-1960s, they were in Memphis, and Phyllis was teaching at Rhodes College, then she was appointed dean of humanities at the Memphis Academy of Art. Over the next decades, Sam had an illustrious career as a pulmonologist. He taught at the University of Tennessee College of Health Sciences, and he practiced privately. Among other noteworthy achievements, Sam diagnosed the first AIDS patient in Memphis in the 1980s, when that disease was still virtually unknown. He went on to care for many AIDS patients, and he and Phyllis have been known for many years in Memphis for their friendship with GLBT persons.

During those years, Phyllis birthed and reared seven children on the farm in Lucy, Tennessee, where they made their home on twenty-ish acres of heaven just outside Memphis. They've known much joy on the farm, where they still reside, as well as some grief—one of their beloved children died in 1970, when he was just days old. With Wade's death, Phyllis left the deanship and turned her eyes toward home.

With others, she started St. Luke's Press in the early 1970s and taught poetry for the Tennessee Arts Commission. By the late 1980s, now a seasoned book publisher, St. Luke's had been acquired by Peachtree Publishers, and they retained Phyllis to run the imprint.

She quit in 1989. She was going home to write. But after just thirteen months, Daisy Marlyes called and asked Phyllis to start a religion department at *Publishers Weekly*, the flagship trade journal of book publishing. There, Phyllis was a pioneer in the long-neglected but now booming area of religious publishing. Across the country and around the world, industry insiders, journalists, and sociologists wanted to know who in the world was buying all these religion books, and they turned to Phyllis for answers.

In 2004, after a dozen years, the neutrality of journalism was chapping Phyllis's hide. She wanted to speak her mind. She wanted not just to report on faith, but also to talk about faith, including her own. And, as much as she respected and even loved other religions, it was her own Christianity that she was most interested in promulgating. Just as she had done with the *Divine Hours* prayer books, the first of which was published in 2000, she then did with her books on the emergence of Christianity.

■ ■ ■

So Phyllis's professional career can be roughly categorized into three periods: (1) a teacher and dean of humanities, (2) a leader in the publishing industry, and (3) an expert in the emergence of the church at the beginning of the twenty-first century. In the first period, her influence was mostly upon students, many of whom are still expressing their gratitude to her today. In the second period, her influence was primarily in the world of publishing professionals, though a couple of her books caught the attention of larger audiences.

It was in the third period of her career—in her writing and speaking about the recovery of ancient spiritual practices and the Great Emergence—that she captured the imagination of the church, writ large.

But that's not to say that she's always been right.

Because we speak on similar topics, Phyllis and I often find ourselves speaking at the same events. Indeed, we've been asked to copresent many times, in venues as dissimilar as the Jesus People's Cornerstone Festival (populated primarily by unwashed, evangelical hard rockers) and the Lenten Series at Calvary Episcopal Church in Memphis (populated by well-washed and well-heeled senior citizens). And, having done these dog-and-pony shows a few times now, we're acutely aware of the areas in which we disagree.

One such area is Phyllis's insistence in nearly every talk she gives that the crowd understand the difference between the *emerging, emergent,* and *emergence* church. To her way of thinking, the lattermost term—which also happens to be her favored term—is the big umbrella under which the others— plus new monasticism, house church, fresh expressions, and alt worship—all cower. *Her* vision is The Great Emergence (With Capital Letters), whilst *our* little emergences are just subsets thereof. She's damn sure she's right, and I think she's full of it.

We've playfully argued this point on numerous occasions, and, though I have made my point convincingly, Phyllis is incorrigible. She is also recalcitrant. And some other words that I can't print. But I love her, and we've laughed uproariously on stage when debating this, much to the bewilderment of audiences.

Others have objected to parts of her work as well. Several reviewers, for example, complained that the every-500-years-rummage-sale argument with which Phyllis begins *The Great Emergence* is too broad a generalization, and that it doesn't hold water with history. Her response has been twofold: (1) Yes, she's said, of course any periodization of history is somewhat unnuanced, and (2) she's written yet another book (forthcoming) about the epochal changes in the church leading to the current

Age of the Holy Spirit. So, she both caveated and doubled-down on her argument.

Others have wondered whether her prophecy that the four quadrants of the church—liturgical, social justice, conservative, and renewalist—will converge into a Christianity of the Great Emergence is merely wishful thinking. Doesn't it instead seem like the increasing hyperindividualization wrought by postmodern technology will instead mean that someday there will be as many denominations as there are Christians? This argument is a bit like astrophysicists arguing about whether the universe will continue to expand or will reach a gravitational limit and collapse back in on itself, commencing another Big Bang cycle. That is, it's pure conjecture. In *The Great Emergence*, Phyllis makes sociological and historical arguments for the convergence that she predicts; in the forthcoming book, *Age of the Spirit*, she and her coauthor Jon M. Sweeney turn to theological arguments, positing that as Christians around the world turn to the "third person" in the Trinity, God's Spirit will begin the grand reunification that Phyllis has been promoting.

No matter if you object to something she's said or written, you've got to admit that Phyllis has been right a lot more than she's been wrong—that goes for her work on "God-talk in America" to the Great Emergence. Plus, she's always got lots of footnotes, so you know she's not pulling this stuff out of thin air.

She also gets away with murder. Between the Southern charm, the white hair, and the culottes, Phyllis Tickle gets to say things to crowds that would get me run out of town on a rail. But when she says it, with a wink and a Tennessean aphorism, people laugh and applaud. Phyllis could tell Job that his house was on fire, his cattle were dead, and his wife had run off with the neighbor, and Job would thank her and ask for boils! That's basically what she's been telling church audiences for years—that the entire way of life that they know, religiously speaking, is coming to an end. But somehow, when they hear it from her, it doesn't seem like doomsday prophecy. From her, it sounds like good news.

She's right. The church is changing, dying and being reborn, right before our eyes. Phyllis has said that in a way no one else has. She's got the *bona fides* to back it up—the footnotes and the life experience. She is equally at ease in front of a crowd and behind a keyboard, plus she's breathtakingly prolific, so her message has been heard far and wide. Her interpretations of the past and her prophecies about the future will be talked about and debated for years to come.

▪ ▪ ▪

Now Phyllis has declared the end to her traveling. After hundreds of days on the road each year, teaching and preaching and cajoling and nagging the church into the future, she's said that she's said enough. At least about that topic. She's coming off the road as this book goes to print, in search of the next thing that will occupy her imagination. In our most recent conversation, she suggested that maybe she'll return to poetry. There have been three major chapters in her professional life, and I don't put it past her to write a fourth.

No matter what she turns her mind to, her six kids, seven grandkids, three great-grandkids, four dogs, ten acres, and Sam are sure to keep her busy. As are we, her myriad friends.

PART

I

PHYLLIS'S
GIFTS
TO
PUBLISHING
AND
THE CHURCH

ONE

BEFORE AMAZON

The Two Women Who Changed
Religious Publishing[1]

Jon M. Sweeney

Before Amazon.com sold its first book in June 1995, two women were transforming spiritual and religious books and the market for them. Those two women were Sallye Leventhal, religion category buyer for the superstores of Barnes & Noble, Inc. (B&N), and Phyllis Tickle, *Publishers Weekly's* founding editor for religion.

I am not sure if Sallye and Phyllis have ever actually met, but I have long been convinced that we in religion publishing owe them a portion of our paychecks. The two of them were not simply in the right place at the right time (although, as they would both surely tell you, they were), they were also brilliant, incisive, prescient, and possessors of boundless enthusiasm. They saw, before and more completely than the rest of us, how books have the power to carry religion and spirituality where churches

---

1. Many thanks to Thomas Grady and Stephen Hanselman for reading and critiquing an earlier version of this essay.

and synagogues, priests, pastors, rabbis, and imams never could. They understood a foundational truth (an old-fashioned term, I realize) encapsulated in a quote from theologian Paul Tillich's Earl Lectures of 1963, used often by Phyllis back in the day: "Hear this one important warning! Never consider the secular realm Godless just because it does not speak of God."[2] And they knew that Karl Popper was wrong when he declared, in 1989, that the ancient Greeks, by creating the first commercial books in the centuries before Christ, did away forever with their sacredness.[3]

SUPERSTORE The Church of Books

Perhaps I should credit Leonard Riggio, the chairman of B&N, rather than Sallye Leventhal, for his visionary creation, or at least his rapid duplication, of "third places," which back then we called by the purely capitalistic name "superstores." (The independent bookstores called them other, less complimentary names.) The success of B&N's Fifth Avenue 150,000-square-foot flagship store led Riggio to believe that people in other parts of the United States—in places with far less to do than in bustling Manhattan—might be attracted to a shopping experience that involves expansive inventory, readily available coffee, magazines and sundries, and large, comfy armchairs. It was after adding many lucrative acquisitions to the B&N fold in the 1980s that the

2. Paul Tillich, *The Irrelevance and Relevance of the Christian Message*, introduction by A. Durwood Foster (Cleveland: Pilgrim Press, 1996), 62.
3. See Appendix to Chapter 7, "On a Little-known Chapter of Mediterranean History," in Karl R. Popper, *In Search of a Better World: Lectures and Essays from Thirty Years* (New York: Routledge, 1996), 107–16.

chairman turned his attention to creating these larger stores. At the time, he was spurred on by the Borders brothers in Michigan, who were doing the same sort of thing, but they never had the quality and efficiency controls of their rivals at B&N.

The superstore was defined as a seriously large bookstore, usually between 50,000 and 150,000 square feet, offering at least 100,000 titles, music selections, a café, and other amenities. They were distinguished from big-box stores, in that *big-box* usually also means a literal box shape, strictly rectangular, and also a single floor of cavernous shopping space, whereas many of the superstore bookstores never fit that mold. They also were not an exclusive creation of B&N and Borders; the "great independents" like Tattered Cover in Denver, Powell's in Portland, and Book-People in Austin come to mind.

By the end of 1989, B&N had 23 superstores across the United States. By 1992, there were more than 100. In the mid-1990s, one superstore on the Upper West Side once enjoyed a fiscal year in which they sold more than $16 million worth of books, music, and videos (it is, as you might guess, now closed). Most superstores were doing $3.5 million a year. By the end of 1995, B&N owned and operated 358 superstores, and by the end of 1997, the company posted annual sales of nearly $2.5 billion. This was the high point for bricks-and-mortar stores selling books in America. The good independents remained strong—stronger, in fact, due to the presence of competition between B&N and Borders. This competition challenged the independents to do a better job of representing a wide spectrum of inventory. By September 1998,

B&N had opened its first superstore on a university campus at the University of Pennsylvania. Penn's then-president, Judith Rodin, was quoted in the school paper saying, "The addition of the Barnes & Noble superstore to our community will dramatically enhance the quality of life on campus. The partnership between one of the best booksellers in the country and one of the nation's leading Ivy League universities will enrich our students, our community and the City of Philadelphia."[4] Those were heady days when a retailer of a much-needed and loved commodity was in sync with the needs of its customers, and its customers were genuinely thankful.

HOW SUPERSTORES BUOYED RELIGIOUS PUBLISHING

Overnight, with the creation of all of this space, the market for books in this country was transformed. The old knock against independent booksellers (and I have been one myself) was that they were idiosyncratic in their tastes, finicky about what they stocked, and notoriously averse to handling religion. It is no secret that the "average" reader—and most people, studies show, are more than willing to call themselves "average"— were intimidated by independent booksellers. Whereas the superstores made no distinction between books worthy of inclusion and merchandising, many people had experiences of walking into an independent bookstore, inquiring after a certain

4. "Barnes & Noble To Build Nation's First University 'Superstore' at Penn," University of Pennsylvania Press Release, April 22, 1996 upenn.edu/almanac/between /bookstor.html accessed Oct 23, 2013

book, and being told in no uncertain terms that it was not, and would never be, stocked there. Before 1990, I would estimate that to nine out of ten independent booksellers, all books dealing with God or prayer or spirituality were deemed "religious," and "religious books" were deemed the proper domain of evangelical bookstores, then known as the Christian Booksellers Association (CBA). Meanwhile, spiritual books (without the word *prayer*, and often replacing *God* with *Goddess*) were to be found in so-called New Age stores. People will go to *those* stores to buy those books, the independent booksellers scornfully believed.

But, of course, they were wrong, and Sallye and Phyllis knew it. It wasn't safe to say it out loud then, but it is now: the superstores of B&N, Borders, and, later, Books-a-Million literally built and sustained the market for religious and spiritual books in this country, perhaps even long after it truly made wise, fiscal sense.[5]

In England, retailers have always been called *stockists*, which puts a fine point on the purpose of retailers in the minds of consumers: places where one can find goods that one may want to purchase. Due to the dramatic growth of superstores in the 1990s throughout the United States, booksellers finally became terrific, efficient stockists. Yes, the superstores hurt the independents, but also yes, the independents, on the whole, were not friendly to religious and spiritual books. As with other categories (e.g., science fiction), the independents needed the superstores to kick them in the pants in order to see that religion and spirituality

5. Now that the superstores are faltering, it's an open question as to whether the finally strengthening independents will change their well-entrenched aversion to the Religion category.

were not going away, but were bursting at the seams in American life. A 2012 *New York Times* story on publishing and bookselling referred to how B&N was "once viewed as the brutal capitalist of the book trade."[6] That's very true. But from a religious publisher's perspective, just as we were sad to see good independents fold, we were simultaneously, and to a far greater extent, grateful for the exponentially increasing shelf space for our category.

In the final analysis, Leonard Riggio built the stores knowing that consumers would come, but it was Sallye Leventhal who stocked them with infectious enthusiasm. Other categories had less enthusiastic managers. Believe me, I was there in those days as the national accounts sales representative for two different publishing houses. You couldn't get the attention of many of the buyers, but Sallye was always sensitive, attentive, and passionate about what her books—the ones in the large Religion sections of those enormous stores—could do in the world. A graduate of Hope College in 1978, she quickly "got it," knowing how important religion and spirituality are to Americans, and how underserved they had been for so long.

GIVING BIRTH TO NEW PUBLISHERS

Consider, for a moment, the small, vital religion trade publishing houses that were born at that time. There were dozens, perhaps hundreds, of all persuasions that started in the late 1980s and throughout the decade of the 90s. For example,

---

6. Julie Bosman, "The Bookstore's Last Stand," *New York Times*, January 29, 2012.

Wisdom Publications decided that they would begin publishing translations of Buddhist sutras and tantras from London, England, in 1987, and then moved to Boston in late 1988. They believed that if readers had the opportunity to find such books, they might even be popular. Who knew? They apparently did, or they guessed—given the climate and the support they could count on from Sallye and Phyllis—and they were right.

Meanwhile, Jewish Lights Publishing, which started in rural Vermont in 1990, became the first publisher dedicated to popular Jewish spirituality. Before Jewish Lights came along, Jewish book publishing meant resources on ritual for rabbis or the synagogue and books on history and the Holocaust for scholars and libraries. The company began simply, bringing a few Lawrence Kushner books back into print that had been dropped by Harper & Row. Jewish Lights—for which I worked in the 1990s—had the idea to create an inspirational literature from Jewish sources "for people of all faiths, all backgrounds." They figured that Christians might even become their largest customer segment if they were given the chance to find such books in bookstores, and to hear about them in the media. They were right, and they flourished.

The great old dames of religion publishing had of course been around for a long time. Doubleday, for example—where, if your book made it into the Image paperback imprint, it meant an in-print and distribution longevity and breadth comparable to ancient Roman Caesars—was founded in 1897 by Frank Nelson Doubleday. In 1910, the company moved operations to Garden City on Long Island, where the City of New York even built the firm its own train station. Image emerged as an imprint in 1954, and it was the domain of Doubleday's mostly Catholic titles. In other words, there were books on and about religion long before Sallye and Phyllis were on the scene, but the market for them, pre-1990, was quite different.

Even a great old publisher like Harper was a part of this demarcation in the market for religious and spiritual books, pre-1990. It was back in 1977 that a dozen employees moved from the New York City offices of Harper & Row and established HarperSanFrancisco (now HarperOne). In those early days, their list was dominated by body-mind-spirit titles, because that was back when, to the vast majority of the book industry, the "Religion" category meant evangelical Christian, and "Spiritual" meant body-mind-spirit. The in-between hadn't yet been discovered.[7]

There were other in-betweens that hadn't yet emerged, as well. Throughout his life, for instance, Fulton J. Sheen published his best-selling books with exclusively Roman Catholic publishing houses such as P. J. Kenedy & Sons and Bruce Publishing Company, which most of us have never heard of today. These books sold millions of copies, but almost exclusively to Catholics. They were reviewed only in Catholic media. They were stocked and sold only in Catholic bookshops, next to holy cards, holy medals, and First Communion dresses. This was all about to change.

---

7. HarperSanFrancisco's founding publisher, Clayton Carlson, is now writing a history of religious publishing.

PHYLLIS COMES ON THE SCENE

Phyllis Tickle was out in the field calling religious and spiritual books "portable pastors" in the late 1980s, watching how other forms of media were beginning to mirror what seemed to be happening in the book business: creating divine space in people's lives. She saw how religious and spiritual books could do for people what they used to have to go to church, synagogue, or zendo to obtain or realize. A decade later, she talked about the success of *The Matrix* on the big screen, but more importantly, what it meant that it sold more copies on DVD than any other movie up until its time. Or the way that a simple television series like *Touched by an Angel* had created such passionate fans, encouraging religious professionals to pay attention and causing an avalanche of angel books to issue from publishing houses. Yes, we can perhaps blame Phyllis for some of those.

The point is that when she talked this way, about such things, Phyllis sparked an entire renaissance. And it *was* a renaissance in religious books and spiritual book publishing from roughly 1990 until 2007. As she was the first to tell us, beginning as the founding religion editor at *Publishers Weekly* on Monday, December 7, 1992, Baker & Taylor's sales of books in religion and spirituality to libraries almost doubled in 1991. And by 1993, Ingram Book Company watched its sales of religious and spiritual books jump by 246 percent in a single fiscal year. The race was on. And as these trends continued, we in the book business created far more books and found many more readers than ever before. Phyllis did not preside over this burgeoning;

she schooled it and fueled it with her passion, intelligence, and articulation. At the outset of *Greed*, Phyllis's powerful little book in the Oxford series on the Seven Deadly Sins, she refers to herself as "a student of religion commercially applied."[8] That she became in December 1992, and thank God.

It used to be that someone like Fulton Sheen sold a million books because the people who heard him on the radio or heard him preach would then purchase his book. But in the 1990s we saw this process change dramatically. The clergy who sold millions of books did so because they picked up on how to communicate with the millions who wanted "portable pastors" more than the flesh-behind-the-pulpit kind. These clergy heard Phyllis, they saw the trend, and thus became the Charles Stanley, Bill Hybels, and T. D. Jakes of the genre.

As Phyllis reported, interpreted, and wrote weekly in the pages of *Publishers Weekly*, readers gained an understanding of the trends in religion that—even though they were a part of them already—they did not fully grasp without Phyllis, how books could help them understand and participate even more in these trends. I am talking about the way in which Phyllis helped us make out such topics as the "quest for the historical Jesus," immersing herself in them, encapsulating and explaining them, in the way that only Phyllis can, as if she were a professional journalist and a scholar. And, of course, she was and is both of those things, and so that didn't require any great trick on

8. Phyllis A. Tickle, *Greed: The Seven Deadly Sins* (New York: Oxford University Press, 2004), 1. The bibliographer in me wants to know why Phyllis used the middle initial of her name on this book. It seems to be the only occasion when she did so.

her part. The *trick*—and I use the word deliberately, to remind you of the image of the "trickster" among native peoples—was Phyllis's enthusiasm. When she lit upon a topic in religion, always with that scholarly hunger, the result was not simple reporting but a sort of magical fuel.

Back to the historical Jesus. Many readers will remember that this subject was at the center of religious and spiritual book publishing for the better part of the 1990s, sparked most of all by a review of John Dominic Crossan's *The Historical Jesus* in the *New York Times Book Review* on December 23, 1991. That review was both a sign and signal that speculation about the historical Jesus had entered a new, vibrant era. In some ways, the current wave of interest in this subject still hasn't ended. And right there at the beginning of it all was Phyllis, tracing a line from Albert Schweitzer to the Jesus Seminar, referring to books and fueling the publishing of more books each step along the way. Are there any publishers reading my words now who don't think Phyllis had the phone numbers of Bob Funk, Marcus Borg, Dom Crossan, Jack Spong, and Tom Wright in the early and mid-1990s on her speed dial or mobile, when the "third quest" was in its heyday?

She presided over the market for religious and spiritual books in the same way that President Bill Clinton presided over the American economy at about that same time—with confidence, intelligence, and enthusiasm. I believe that the comparison is apt: just as we had a supreme cheerleader-in-chief in the White House boosting the GNP, we had a similar figure working for the religious and spiritual book business always somewhere between her home in Lucy, Tennessee, and her hotel room in New York City. Phyllis once self-deprecatingly declared that this sort of thing, on her part, was usually "98 percent ham and 2 percent information," but that, I think, was a bit of misplaced modesty.[9]

NO FAVORITISM HERE

With her energy for learning and communicating what she knows, Phyllis fueled dozens of other vital conversations burning in religion and spiritual life. Chaos theory and chance. The appropriation of Eastern religious practice into Western religions—appropriate assimilation, or just the latest form of imperialism? Zen Catholics. Kabbalah for everyone (Madonna, oy!). Ecumenism, interfaith, multifaith, and what they all mean. Why do people look for religion in spiritual books, and what does this trend mean for the future of faith and organized religion? Womanist theology. Mujerista theology. The environmental revolution and what it means for God and the Earth. Changes in the language that we use for God. Changes in the language that we use to describe ourselves in relation to God. The rapprochement of East and West in Christianity. The rapprochement of Judaism and Christianity. Christian hunger to learn about the Jewishness of Jesus—who knew? (Phyllis did, even before Rob Bell.) The rediscovery of mysticism and meditation as native within Judaism. The impact of the Global South on Westernized or

9. Phyllis Tickle, *Prayer Is a Place: America's Religious Landscape Observed* (New York: Doubleday, 2005), 46.

Latinized religion. The growth of Islam worldwide. Gnosticism and other secrets. "The pursuit of truth through the acceptance of mystery."[10] No wonder Phyllis loved her job. This list could go on forever.

She brought the same energy to what Phyllis herself came to call the Great Emergence, when she finally left the journalism of *Publishers Weekly* and took on the role of prognosticator. She'd been talking about emergence Christianity as early as 2001, as far as I can tell, referring to experts like historian John Lukacs. Well, now Phyllis is the expert whom they all quote.

Then, of course, Phyllis's impact was doubled—or quadrupled—whenever she spoke on radio, TV, in congregations, and at conferences, because she brought a wealth of knowledge and insight to the ways in which religion is alive and changing, and she inspired people wherever she went. And she went a lot of places. It is often said that the Great Reformation wouldn't have spread with the velocity that it did were it not for the invention of the printing press a few decades earlier. This is certainly true. The printing press, and the books that it rapidly created in large numbers, spread Luther's and Erasmus's radical ideas not so much like manure fertilizing fields, but as dust to the winds. But there were good editors then, too, behind the scenes interpreting, distilling, explaining, and propagating the ideas coming off the presses in ink. The Great Reformation needed them as much as it

---

10. Ibid., 116. This phrase is one among hundreds of possible examples of how Phyllis's reporting inspired publishers' marketing departments, if not also their editorial acquisition colleagues, to quote her without attribution.

needed Luther himself. Similarly, scholars have written about the role of newspapers in the American colonies, spreading Thomas Paine's words like wildfire, fueling the American Revolution. Paine's pamphlets were not enough; newspaper editors showed the American populace how to use those ideas to create a revolution. In the great renaissance of spirituality and religion of the 1990s, we had Phyllis.

CONVERGING PATHS

My own career in publishing began in the fall of 1993, a few months after I'd left bookselling behind in Cambridge, Massachusetts, to become Augsburg Fortress's Trade Sales Representative for the southeastern United States. After a summer of calling on bookstores throughout Tennessee, Georgia, Virginia, Alabama, the Carolinas, and Florida (where one CBA retailer took one look at my camel hair jacket in July and said, "You aren't really from around here, now are you?"), I was off to the American Academy of Religion (AAR)/Society of Biblical Literature (SBL) annual meetings in Washington, DC. The AAR and SBL are two guilds of academics specializing in religion, and together they comprise nearly 10,000 religion professors. This gathering was the highlight of our year at Fortress Press, and my first time working AAR/SBL was a week that I will never forget.

The 1993 gathering of AAR/SBL was also Phyllis's first as the founding religion editor for *Publishers Weekly*. I remember seeking her out in a café, where she sat with a colleague sipping something warm, probably intending to be away from scrutiny for a while, and asking her a question about the industry. I cannot remember what the question was, precisely, but I stated an opinion and asked Phyllis what she thought of it. "I think you're right on, Mr. Sweeney!" she shot back at me. Buoyed, as she has buoyed so many of us in our careers in books and religion, I went my way believing that I was clever, and that the future was bright for all of us. I wasn't, and it was.

She still does inspire and inform me, and us, of course, and one of the purposes of this book is to mark the fact that, perhaps now, as she turns eighty, Phyllis may someday soon slow down. Surely, this will happen, sometime, eventually. The contributors to these pages cannot replace her—no one can—but I know that she's inspired them to carry on her good work. May it happen.

TWO

"SHE JUST STICKS HER ARMS OUT, NO MATTER WHO'S COMING"

Phyllis Tickle and the Practice of Holy Envy

Jana Riess

Back in my twenties, before I had a public blog and had published books on the Church of Jesus Christ of Latter-day Saints, only a couple of things on my CV hinted that Mormonism might be my own personal faith, including the subject matter of my dissertation (Protestant women missionaries who went to Utah in the late nineteenth century to try to save Mormon women from polygamy) and the fact that I had presented papers at the Mormon History Association's annual meeting. So I hoped the question wouldn't arise when, at the age of twenty-nine, I went to interview for my dream job as the religion book review editor of *Publishers Weekly* magazine.

I had excellent reasons for hoping that the subject of Mormonism would not come up. I'd had a number of sad experiences of other people's anti-Mormon prejudices—even well-educated people whom I would have expected to be more tolerant. Some had told me that Mormonism was a cult, that I clearly could not think for myself, and that it was a perversion of true Christianity. At my husband's Methodist church, the congregation decided to hold a six-week series on "cults in America," with Exhibit A being Mormonism. All the old anti-Mormon tropes were taught in the class, from the idea that Mormons believe they will be gods in the afterlife to an enumeration of reasons why the Book of Mormon could not possibly be scripture. Some of the women in my Bible study went to the class, women I thought were friends; one of them e-mailed me afterward to announce that the beliefs I held were clearly not compatible with the biblical Christianity she knew to be true, and to tell me she didn't think we could be friends anymore.

I cried. And my husband eventually became an Episcopalian.

So given that people have a tendency to hear the word *Mormon* and assume all sorts of things based on that lone fact, I prayed it would not be an issue with the job interview, and it basically wasn't. But after I had gotten the position, negotiated a salary and start date, and met some of my new colleagues, one of them—a sparkling-eyed lady named Phyllis Tickle— asked me point-blank what my own religion was. I figured that I already had the job at that point, so it was time to lay my cards on the table.

"I'm a Mormon," I said, waiting for the usual uncomfortable silence. Instead, what I got was Phyllis clapping her hands together and saying, "Oh, good! We need more religious diversity on our staff."[11]

What a welcome surprise that was to me. Phyllis seemed genuinely delighted that I was Mormon. To her, it was not a handicap for me to overcome by slowly proving myself as some sort of exponent of a "model minority." Rather, it was a strength, something she believed would add variety and a fresh perspective to our ranks.

Over many years of working with Phyllis, I came to understand that the hospitality with which she welcomed me was the rule, not the exception. The way she encounters other faiths, and other traditions within her own Christian faith, has become a model for me. What I share here—based on my own interactions with Phyllis, some stories she tells in her writings, and the recollections of some of her friends and colleagues—are four ways I think that Phyllis's approach can serve as a model for all of us as we approach religions that are different from, or even in opposition to, our own.

1. ACTIVELY SEEK THE GOOD . . .

I have told people many times that it is a dream of my life to become the person that Phyllis Tickle believes me to be. She has been known to send me the most over-the-top, ridiculous e-mails about how talented I am, how kind, how smart, etc. "Whatever it is that blooms inside you, Jana, it is good for all of us, just being

---

11. Months later, another staff member told me that her own reaction was equally as positive, but for a very different reason: "Oh, good! We need a designated driver."

able to see it and be near it," she wrote me once. Can you imagine? I knew this was ludicrous praise when I read it, and yet in the days afterward I also knew it was forming me into something *more;* I may not have been blooming before the words were written but I certainly felt a mandate to bloom after reading them. That was and is Phyllis's gift.

It's not just that Phyllis sees the best in individual people; it's that she looks for the best even in the flawed religious institutions those individuals inhabit. When approaching something new or different, she begins from the assumption that she is going to feel what Krister Stendahl calls "holy envy" for each religion she encounters.[12] She expects this. She *wants* to be shaken up, even transformed, when encountering a new religion. How many of us can say the same?

When Phyllis came on board at *Publishers Weekly* six years before I did, she realized she needed to shore up not only her knowledge of world religions but her personal experience of them. She and her executive editor and dear friend, Daisy Maryles, had together decided that coverage in the magazine was "going to have to be all religions equally," and that doing so required some education. For example, what little Phyllis knew about Islam came from books, and she confessed that she was

12. Krister Stendahl's three rules for interfaith understanding are: "Let the other define herself ('Don't think you know the other without listening'); compare equal to equal (not my positive qualities to the negative ones of the other); and find beauty in the other so as to develop 'holy envy.'" See Yehezkel Landau, "An Interview with Krister Stendahl," *Harvard Divinity Bulletin* 35, no. 1 (Winter 2007), accessed online at http://www.hds.harvard.edu/news-events/harvard-divinity-bulletin/articles/an -interview-with-krister-stendahl on November 11, 2013.

"not overly fond" of what she did know.[13] So at the 1993 World Parliament of Religions in Chicago, she set out to change that— and I say "set out" because there was nothing accidental about it. She went to that conclave with the understanding that she did not know enough about Islam, and that what she thought she knew might be wrong.

She attended a demonstration of Sufi whirling dervishes because it was one of the only sessions on the program that hinted at Islam in practice, which is what she felt she needed to see, even though she knew that Sufism is not typically regarded as representative of Islam more generally. Phyllis was entranced by the dance and music, allowing herself to be carried "wherever it was we were going to go":

> When I had started to cry, I do not know. It doesn't matter. I had never seen ecstatic worship before, never understood before that the human body is light and its God a consuming fire from which it emanates and to which it returns with erotic ferocity when it frees itself to know itself.
>
> Oh, God . . . God . . . God. It is all about God. That's all any of it has ever been about and all it ever will be. They're not religions, they're ways to the center where the body flames up and the dervishes whirl.[14]

We see in this account that Phyllis came to regard Sufism as more than just another path to God. Being open to beauty and

13. Phyllis Tickle, *Prayer Is a Place: America's Religious Landscape Observed* (New York: Doubleday, 2005), 37.
14. Ibid., 62–63.

truth wherever it appeared, she found Sufism unexpectedly, crushingly beautiful, causing her to rethink her own style of worship *and* the purpose of religion in general.

Holy envy indeed.

2. . . . WHILE CALLING 'EM AS YOU SEE 'EM

Being ecumenical and practicing holy envy don't require being a pushover. I remember from my days at *Publishers Weekly* that Phyllis always knew how to call things as she saw them (and she would often do so with some unforgettable Southernism). Let's face it: some religious people are genuine, some are hucksters, and some are just plum crazy. And aside from individual variation, there are some religious ideas that we are going to actively disagree with. Phyllis, for example, once told me that there was one particular religion that we were called to cover at the magazine to which she had a serious biblical objection. But she was aware of that prejudice on her part and never allowed it to affect how she did her job.

One thing Phyllis can't tolerate is demagoguery, whether it's within her own religious tradition or someone else's.[15] One story she recounts in *Prayer Is a Place* speaks to her determination not to give quarter to hero-worship, even if the object of said reverence is someone so universally beloved as the Dalai Lama. Criticizing His Holiness in our day and age is akin to kicking a puppy or declaring that unicorns and rainbows should die; it simply isn't done. And yet she did it.

15. I can only imagine her cringing at the obsequious tone of a Festschrift, to take a purely hypothetical example.

At a professional meeting in the 1990s, Phyllis was privileged to be invited to a special closed session with the Dalai Lama, with about 125 people in attendance. After waiting long past the appointed time, she was horrified when he (finally) appeared and the small crowd showed obeisance by every possible measure:

> I have had to wonder a thousand times since that Friday if my sense of disgust was a matter of cultural distaste or of religious conviction. Either way, I was not any happier with my own reaction to all the bobbing heads and bending bodies than I was with appearing to be the only person in the room who, albeit standing in respect, was not worshipping . . . for that is what was happening.[16]

How, she wondered, could he possibly allow this display? How could he endure it? For endure it he had—"had empowered even, and apparently enjoyed." Phyllis was appalled by it all, right down to the spiritual guru's Rolex watch and designer eyeglasses.

But in typical Phyllis-fashion, the story is not so clear-cut as all that. Because the other possibility—beyond the obvious conclusion that he was "a very skillful and informed opportunist playing on the gullibility of crowd mentality"—was that the Dalai Lama actually was who the crowd believed him to be. Humbled, she was reminded of another triumphal entry:

> Oh, God!
> Had the doors not been locked, I am sure I would have fled out of that place, half drunk for air. I have no idea how my

16. Tickle, *Prayer Is a Place*, 72.

understanding of Buddhism has been affected over the years since by that single minute of epiphany, but I've got a fairly sound notion of how my perception of Christianity has, for it took on a messy but vivid historicity for me at that exact moment. Real people had done this same thing once in Jerusalem, and it had been permitted then too, permitted by the one whom I worship as God. Either He is and knew Himself to be, or . . .

In either case, "Oh, God!"[17]

Here Phyllis is not afraid to censure idolatry, if what happened was indeed idolatry. But she also—and this is the crux of the matter—holds out the tantalizing possibility that the Dalai Lama could endure the praise only because as a divine personage he was worthy of it. What's more, she finds that the lesson of that historical moment, for her, was to bring her own faith home in a singular way.

3. STAY IN RELATIONSHIP

I don't recall ever having had a conversation with Phyllis about how to "do" ecumenism. I don't remember discussing theoretical models of interfaith dialogue with her, though I'm sure when we were both at *Publishers Weekly* there were many books that crossed our desks on that very subject. I don't imagine that Phyllis spends a lot of time and energy reading about theoretical paradigms for how to talk to people of other religions. She simply talks to them.

17. Ibid., 73.

What this says to me is that good ecumenism, real ecumenism, is about relationships. Relationships come first and everything else is sixth or maybe twenty-sixth. Phyllis's ecumenism is situational, arising organically from the friendships she forms with such apparent ease. I'm not sure she had known many other Mormons before she met me, but as I relayed in this chapter's opening anecdote, she was immediately ready not only to receive me but to posit that I was not merely a "credit to my religion"—an apparent compliment that is actually an insult. Being a credit to your race or religion or sexual orientation means that you are an exception to the rule, but that the "rule" as society has preconceived it still stands, whether it's that Mormons are idiots, Jews are greedy, or Muslims are violent. When Phyllis began working with me, she assumed that my being Mormon would somehow make a great contribution to the staff, providing, as she put it in her memoir, an "extra beneficence" to our work together.[18]

Phyllis begins with the notion that relationships come before dogma, before ideology, before who is "right" and who is "wrong." This came into play in the late 1990s when she and Sam got involved in Holy Trinity Community Church in Memphis, known for its "all-inclusive" approach to homosexuality. Their decision was not overtly political so much as it was about the people:

> In becoming congregants of Holy Trinity, Sam and I did
> what we did not out of any desire to take a position on one
> side or the other of a well-wedged issue. Rather, we did what

18. Ibid., 294.

we did out of the sure knowledge that we at last had found our place in the larger kingdom of God; and we have not looked back since.[19]

Phyllis wrote those words in the early 2000s, and since that time she and Sam have moved to another congregation. A couple of years ago, they began attending Christ City Church in Memphis, which might seem a surprising choice for an Episcopalian with moderate-to-liberal leanings. Pastor Jonathan McIntosh describes the congregation as "fairly conservative," which includes conservative stances on homosexuality and women in ministry; after all, the church has its early roots in the Acts 29 Network associated with Mark Driscoll. However, the congregation is also deeply committed to social justice and serving the city.

The friendship that Jonathan has struck up with Phyllis and Sam may seem unlikely on the surface, but not to people who know Phyllis and understand the primacy she puts on relationships. She brings Jonathan to her house, where she and Sam host regular dinners and gatherings with their LGBTQ friends. "Sam and Phyllis are a hub for gays in their town, so whenever you go to dinner there, there are different gay men and lesbians that they are helping, people who have a lot of wounds," Jonathan says. "Their house is almost like a safe haven." He has been changed theologically by the fellowship:

Our conversations helped me solidify that even a conservative church theologically should advocate for the rights of people we disagree with. A conservative church has

19. Ibid., 303.

the responsibility to stand up for anyone who is oppressed. Those conversations have been helpful for me. I continue to be provoked, encouraged, and disturbed as I talk with Phyllis and her friends.[20]

In those conversations, he and Phyllis disagree, sometimes sharply, but he never feels "excluded or manipulated" by her. She expects that he will be true to himself and she will be true to herself, but that they can still be good friends in spite of their disagreements. In today's polarized world, I wonder how many Christians behave similarly.

4. RECOGNIZE THAT OTHERS HAVE A CLAIM ON YOU

One of the things that I most admire about Phyllis is the generosity of time and attention she lavishes on people. *Everyone* thinks they're her best friend, and for that matter they probably are; she knows how to welcome the stranger. Part of that, I have discovered, is that she operates with the assumption that strangers have a legitimate claim on her time.

Carol Showalter, a member of the ecumenical Community of Jesus on Cape Cod, first sought Phyllis out because she had heard her speak and had a spiritual prompting to invite her to the Community. So out of the blue she essentially tackled Phyllis at a trade show and, after a cursory self-introduction, invited her for a visit. Carol remembers:

> I said, "You just *must* come to the Community of Jesus. Can you come? Can you come visit the Community of Jesus

20. Jonathan McIntosh, telephone interview by Jana Riess, July 2, 2013.

on Cape Cod?" And I remember her taking out her date book and saying, "Well, I think I actually could." When I look back on that now, knowing how busy she is, I know how amazing that was. She came within about five weeks, I think.[21]

What ensued from that unexpected conversation was that Phyllis became intimately involved in the life of the Community and an editorial adviser to its publishing arm, Paraclete Press. And the relationships she has forged there have borne fruit in the forms of books, dramas, and liturgy—all of which were made possible because Phyllis said yes when most people in their right mind would have said no. She was open to relationship.

Another of Phyllis's longstanding friendships has been with *Publishers Weekly*'s Daisy Maryles, as mentioned above. Now retired, Daisy has fond memories of the years she spent covering religion with Phyllis and the rest of our eventual team. Apparently this bond was cemented one weekend a decade ago when Daisy and two other New York friends trekked to Tennessee for a sojourn with Sam and Phyllis. After picking the three up from the airport, Sam went home to make Sabbath preparations while Phyllis took the visitors to Graceland, as ecumenical a sacred site as one could hope for. When they returned to the farm, they saw that Sam had kosherized the Tickles' decidedly nonkosher kitchen by spreading sheets of plastic on every counter and surface, using spanking-new pots and pans, and laying out paper plates and plastic utensils. No

---

21. Carol Showalter, interview by Jana Riess, May 3, 2013, Orleans, Massachusetts.

detail was unimportant in ensuring that Daisy, an Orthodox Jew, felt at home come Friday evening.[22]

Daisy had brought a kosher Sabbath meal with deli food, challah, wine, and candles with her from New York, a veritable feast that started at sundown and continued long after Phyllis had left the table for her requisite horizontal down time before bed. After the Sabbath had ended the next evening (and after the group went to Beale Street for jazz and drinks), Daisy came with Sam and Phyllis to church on Sunday. She recalls that Phyllis was anxious that going to church would make Daisy uncomfortable, but Daisy responded that as long as she didn't have to kneel or take communion, she'd be fine. And Phyllis's church (at the time, Holy Trinity), with its openness about gay and lesbian members, made an impression on Daisy. "I learned from this," she says. "In my synagogue, even my modern Orthodox synagogue, I don't know if we could have been that open." Overall, the whole weekend was about mutuality. As Daisy recalls:

> I think it was an open interaction. I don't think it was done for politeness' sake. It was very genuine on everyone's part. We had such a great group of people. It's not that I suddenly said, "Oh, I want your life," or she said, "Oh, I want yours," but we both enjoyed the experience of being in the other person's life for a time. We loved it.[23]

22. Sam had even, upon learning at the airport that Daisy was allergic to cats, hightailed it back to the farm in Lucy to change all the linens and close off her room. That wasn't an overtly religious act, and yet it was; as Daisy put it later, "That just shows you how welcoming they are."
23. Daisy Maryles, telephone interview by Jana Riess, July 1, 2013.

What strikes me about this story of a magical weekend is that each of these friends understood what was vital to the other and took pains to be part of it, whether that was Daisy's attendance at Phyllis's beloved church or the Tickles's carefully planned hospitality so that Daisy would have a comfortable and memorable Sabbath in their home. This, then, is what an ecumenical spirit requires. It is personal and it is effortful. It requires an investment. And it assumes that the other party has a claim on you.

This last observation is the foundation. Phyllis begins with the assumption that when she deals with other people's religions, what is required of her is not a mild tolerance (which in most people actually masks an underlying indifference) but an active engagement. She believes that she is expected to get involved somehow, not just permit that other faith tradition to go its own merry way.

In 1999, the First Church of Christ, Scientist, contacted Phyllis to see if she would like to be part of a bold initiative it was undertaking to build the Mary Baker Eddy Library for the Betterment of Humanity in Boston. The library was going to be a publicly accessible repository for all of the papers of Mrs. Eddy, the founder of Christian Science, whose writings had been partially restricted for nearly a century. Moreover, it sought to become a world-class center for the study of women in nineteenth-century religion more generally. Could Phyllis lend her expertise to its inaugural board of advisers?

There were surely many good reasons to refuse, including a ridiculously busy schedule and a few book contracts in the wings. But frankly, I doubt that Phyllis ever seriously considered saying no. I believe this because I saw her in action with the Christian Scientists. Within a couple of years of her own involvement with the library, she had scored for me a plum assignment writing the introduction and annotations to a never-before-released 1901 autobiography of Mrs. Eddy. I was delighted with the work, since I had done some research on women in early Christian Science back in graduate school, and grateful to Phyllis for helping me make the connection. But I realized throughout those months of research trips to Boston and lovely interactions with the Christian Scientists I met that I had agreed to the project because I could further my academic interests while also getting paid—a rare serendipity for researchers—and not primarily because I felt a kind of moral imperative to learn about another religious tradition for its followers' sake.

That was my failing. I contrast this to Phyllis, who took a lot of heat from fellow Protestants (and from secular journalists) about her public engagement with Christian Science. She stuck with it not because she agreed with the religion, but because she loved the people and believed that their proposed library had a claim on her:

> I am not a Christian Scientist, nor will I ever be. As I have several times remarked to my hosts and colleagues at that Church, I stoutly disagree with several of the scriptural

assumptions or interpretations on which Christian Science and its practices rest. That does not mean, though, that I disagree with the importance of a great library or with that library's perfect right to expect from me whatever I can bring to its furtherance.[24]

A "perfect right to expect from me whatever I can bring to its furtherance": I find that stunning. Most of us don't consecrate that to our *own* religious institutions, let alone the institutions of other faiths.

I've benefited from Phyllis's idea of commitment myself. Some years ago, I became involved in a roundtable discussion on the Book of Mormon at Brigham Young University. A small coterie of Mormon scholars would meet each summer and present papers on various aspects of the text. I don't remember there being any non-Mormons at first. That's not because they would not have been welcome, but because we hadn't encountered scholars of other faiths (or no faith) who were even remotely interested in reading a book that Mark Twain once famously called "chloroform in print." The Book of Mormon was not high on the reading list of non-Latter-day Saints scholars.

Except for Phyllis. I think that the invitation for her to participate arose out of one of the many conversations she and I had about my faith; I don't remember the details. But she traveled at least twice out to Utah for these meetings because, as she said, she had not a personal interest so much as an obligation to learn about Mormonism's sacred text:

24. Tickle, *Prayer Is a Place*, 305.

There was a time, no doubt, in a less globalized, less intimately populous, less information-saturated world when the beliefs of twelve million of our fellow human beings could be considered of little or no relevance to the other millions of us. The times for such arrogance are long gone . . . or pray God, may they be. The individuals and groups within humanity determine the whole. We are in aggregate both what we believe and what our fellows believe; and we can know each other in peace and affection only as we know with respect and accuracy what each corps of us clings to as its foundational text.[25]

Phyllis felt that Mormonism had a claim on her attention not just because she and I were friends and colleagues but also because the religion—then at twelve million adherents and now approaching fifteen—had reached a tipping point of social import.

Phyllis's determination to look for the good while never compromising her own beliefs, her commitment to relationships over ideology, and her openness to the idea that strangers have a claim on her have all become models for me as I navigate a world of complex religious pluralism. How will I respond to the Other? Maybe my first step is to stop imagining that the Other is Other—to be more like Phyllis in putting relationships first. As her long-time friend and fellow Tennessee writer Robert Benson put it, "I can't imagine her ever walking away from someone, no matter what window they're looking through. I can't imagine her being

---

25. Phyllis Tickle, foreword to *The Book of Mormon: Selections Annotated & Explained*, by Jana Riess (Woodstock, VT: SkyLight Paths, 2005), vii.

anything other than open to, not just tolerant of, people who see differently." Benson insists there's no one with whom she can't have a whiskey and a conversation. "She just sticks her arms out, no matter who's coming."[26]

26. Robert Benson, telephone interview by Jana Riess, July 2, 2013.

THREE

WHAT LIES BENEATH

Phyllis Tickle's Voice in Poetic Chancel Drama

Sister Danielle Dwyer

Phyllis Tickle blazes with passion when she talks about drama in the church. She seems to thrive on writing drama that unites Old Testament and New Testament voices. I think this must come from her love of history and her pulse on the church's repeated patterns of need and change. So, finding a voice from the past that will nourish and inspire hope in the future is almost effortless. I would say after working with Phyllis on two of her plays, fueling the church through poetic chancel drama is one of her singular burdens.

I am a member of the Community of Jesus, an ecumenical Christian community in the Benedictine monastic tradition, located in Orleans, Massachusetts. Phyllis has been a friend and colleague for almost twenty years. She has been heavily involved in our publishing company, Paraclete Press, as an active voice and participant on the editorial board. She has also been involved in theater, working with Elements Theatre Company. I am the artistic director of that company and would like to share some of what I know of Phyllis as playwright and poet.

My first time working with Phyllis came in the fall of 2000. Phyllis had already been involved on several Paraclete book projects, and she and her husband, Sam, were invited to join us for a June weekend, celebrating the dedication of our church, a new basilica built in an ancient style. Up to this point, I had only heard of her work, and the stories, honestly, both thrilled and terrified me. How would I work with this woman whose velocity of thought seemed to leave a trail of dust in its path?

To mark the occasion of the church dedication, a few of us wrote and then performed a play in the style of the medieval miracle plays of western Europe. Since it was of that style, we performed it outdoors in front of the church on a wagon-styled stage (complete with a jester!). It had historical roots, scriptural basis, and a relevant and particular message for the day, points that all hit home with Phyllis. And, little did I know, issues relevant to Phyllis's own personal theater work. Phyllis loved the experience of the play and told me it was at this point that her dream to revisit chancel drama emerged in force.[27] I found out later that Phyllis had already made a decision that we would do her play *Figs and Fury* in this newly dedicated space.

---

27. Chancel drama is a style developed for the sacred space of the chancel area in a church. The word *chancel* derives from the French, which in turn came from the late Latin word *cancelli*, meaning lattice. This referred to the screens that separated the nave from the chancel area, the liturgical space often used to celebrate the Eucharist.

Figs and Fury is a chancel drama based on the life of the prophet Jeremiah. We performed it in November 2001, approximately fifteen months after she'd seen our play. The uniqueness of our basilica requires some explanation. The basilican-style church is based on the Roman meetinghouse: a space made for oratory, not so much for quick dialogue. The church is approximately 175 feet long and 60 feet wide. Not your typical theater space.

Figs and Fury was originally commissioned in 1976 by Grace-St. Luke's Episcopal Church in Memphis to celebrate the US bicentennial year. It had been played in the intervening years in churches throughout the English-speaking world. Working with a script written for a specific purpose and for a specific church provided us with some challenges. The acoustic needs in our church were completely different from those of the original space, and we were a very different company of actors than Phyllis had worked with on the original production. We were a young and relatively inexperienced theater company, though few of us were aware of this at the time. I give great credit to Phyllis for her openness to change things as she listened to the actors. While some things had to stay for the sake of the story and the structure of the play, there was a lot of humility on Phyllis's part as we tromped through this play about a prophet she admired greatly.

Early in the process, there was one particular rehearsal worth recounting. Due to where we were in construction of the basilica, our walls were still bare, and that made the reverberation of the spoken human voice quite terrible. At the time, Phyllis seemed almost electrically charged with the task of helping us overcome the reverberation problem. "We are going to conquer it!" she declared at our first reading. "We will read at a pace in which every word can be heard." Groans among the acting troupe were inaudible, but present. After a three-and-a-half-hour reading of a one-hour-long play, we all looked at each other and wanted to cry. This just seemed to charge Phyllis all the more. As she left for Tennessee, her parting words to me were, "Sister D, we *have* to make this work—theater must be an active voice in this church!" These were my sentiments as well—I just wasn't sure how to get us there. Sometimes a push from the outside is what's needed.

While Phyllis was back in Tennessee, we began working with a voice coach. He came down to Cape Cod for the weekends, and not only did we find the life of the voice in the play, but also we found it in the peculiar space that is our beloved basilica. We broke the back of how to speak in the church and made friends with the reverberation. This made all the difference in the performance, and it made subsequent chancel drama possible in the church—which was one of Phyllis's original intents.

JEREMIAH IN OUR MIDST

As we continued to work on the play that summer and fall, our nation was devastated. The 9/11 attacks came right in the middle of our rehearsals. At a time when we were stunned and we were asking why these attacks had happened, we were working intimately with this prophet's words. Jeremiah's indefatigable love for

God and belief in God's goodness inspired us in dark moments that fall and gave us hope in troubling times. These words of the prophet were especially meaningful: "'For I know the plans I have for you,' declares the LORD, 'plans to prosper you and not to harm you, plans to give you hope and a future.'"[28] We got to know each other, and at Phyllis's instigation, Midrash[29] became part of our regular conversation. She introduced us to many Jewish sayings and stories and came to love and respect the fierceness of a poet-prophet who would not be satisfied with mere obedience.

In the last few weeks before the performance, Phyllis began attending rehearsals. Like most playwrights, she was protective of her work, but not possessive. I was worried about how this production would turn out, knowing the passion Phyllis felt for her creation. There was much at stake: the first drama in our new church by a fairly young theater company, a new and acoustically challenging basilica, and the desire to bring to life a relatively challenging text. Were we up to the task?

To say there were a few tense moments will suffice. Both in the preparation and in the performance, live theater is never without moments when disaster is just a hair's breadth away. However, all went well—Jeremiah graced the space and I believe we did Phyllis proud. The still new and unfinished space welcomed into its walls the stories and poetry of the prophet like water into thirsty ground. Chancel drama has the ability to reach out in a naked way to hungry people and

28. Jeremiah 29:11 (NIV).
29. Midrash is a Hebrew tradition of interpreting or explaining Scripture that involves questioning and storytelling.

provide another kind of manna. I believe Phyllis saw this and felt the burden to provide nourishment. We joined in—and became richer for it.

THE DOORWAY OPENS FOR MORE CHANCEL DRAMA

After a successful joint venture with *Figs and Fury,* Phyllis was eager to do more theater with us. She was hatching a plan for multiple Old Testament plays to be written and performed. Unfortunately, we had projects on the docket we couldn't change, so we talked about something in the future. That something in the future took quite a bit of time to materialize. In the meantime, Phyllis took on the mantle of an unofficial sponsor of chancel drama and the possibility of its coming back as an active form of worship.

It was not until the fall of 2007 that the next project materialized. Phyllis was asked by our prioress to write a play for the church's tenth anniversary. It needed to include the moment of Jesus's Transfiguration, as our church is named after that event. This play would be the centerpiece of the weekend celebration marking ten years in our church and the completion of its extensive art program.

After some talk about the play, it became evident that Phyllis needed to spend some time in the church, since it had changed considerably in the seven years since we had produced *Figs and Fury.* Phyllis visited the church three different times, listened to the space, and left feeling she had heard it and knew what it wanted. Her respect for sacred spaces and the prayers and lives of the people in that space seemed to inspire her writing. She speaks about this in an interview about the play:

> In terms of liturgical drama, a signatory piece written for one space was not originally our intention, but that is what this became. . . . It celebrates the structure, enhancing the teaching aspect of the space, but beyond that, it welds or melds the spirit of the people who worship there. This can't just be done with words; it must be aesthetic and experiential. It's very close to what happens when a space has been prayed in through the centuries—when you walk in you just get a sense of it. . . .

> I went into the church alone three times. Finally, I lay down on the floor on the western side of the ambo, and just shut up for 30 or 40 minutes. It had been so long since *Figs and Fury*, I wandered around to see sight lines and things. At first I wanted to use the windows as boxes with shutters for the players to come and go, but this evolved too.

> That space is a womb composed of stuff and story. It has its own story, and it wants to tell its own story, not traveling around. That is a defining characteristic or circumstance of a major religious site, and this space demands that recognition. And the doorway of the church itself is the passageway that enables or enhances that storytelling—like the birth canal between the secular and ecclesial world.[30] [31]

30. "Ecclesial world," meaning the world and tradition of church hierarchy and custom.
31. The full text of this private interview can be found at elementstheatre.org/plays/past/the-doorway/#news_reviews, accessed October 31, 2013.

These ideas and this philosophy play a large part in Phyllis's writing. It obviously influenced her in the original work of *Figs and Fury* for Grace-St. Luke, and in the process of *The Doorway*, as the drama on the Transfiguration was to become known. As a theater director, I find an awareness of space, of the elements needed to create another world, and of the community that you are serving are essential. You must know your audience and why there is a need for such a story. Phyllis began the process of *The Doorway* with all of this awareness in tow.

The work of refining the story and script for *The Doorway* was tedious, requiring several attempts, but what we always agreed on was that the voice of the church had to ring clearly throughout the story.

When we landed on what we both felt was the right story, we came up with two main characters. The first was an artist, Madeleine, which seemed appropriate as all the art was being finished and the church had been inhabited by artists for the last ten years. The second was an owl. Theodore the Owl had a dubious beginning—this was at the height of Harry Potter's popularity, and both of us worried that Harry Potter and his owl, Hedwig, were too much in our consciousness. But neither of us could part with this idea. Then we found two owls in the church mosaic floor and trusted that the church had spoken again.

The poet in Phyllis flourished in the creation of the play. With an artist and an owl that had divine powers as the two main characters, the doors were open to explore the "magic" of the divine, to suspend disbelief, bringing inanimate beings to life, and letting the voice of the poet reign supreme. The poetry especially found its voice in the chorus that was represented by the four elements and had the strongest voice of all.

Phyllis was also given the daunting task of bringing some of the stories of the frescoes to life. She had many themes to weave together. Then, she needed to bring in the story of the Transfiguration. She did all we asked, keeping intact the dignity of the Scripture, the context of the space, and the whimsy needed to allow the audience to enter another world while physically rooted in their own.

The final script was completed three months before the anniversary weekend. During the greater part of the rehearsal process, Phyllis was 1,300-plus miles away and would receive photo updates on the set, the costumes, the rehearsal process, and the music written especially for the piece.

Artists working together can be messy, tense, and painful, and I am very happy to say that we all parted as friends. Phyllis brought to the process her wish to serve the church and the expression of story in this specific space. She was away for much of the working time on the script, and she allowed the play, her child, at times to be brought up by another parent. And when she saw it again, she loved the child all the more for how it had grown. This humility was a great lesson to me, and I know it was to others in the company as well.

Phyllis continues her work at Paraclete Press on the editorial board. She continues to invite discussion on the needs of the church at large and how to respond to them both with a new and a historical face. Phyllis also continues her involvement with Elements Theatre Company, and her next project with us will be adapting one of Charles Dickens's novels for the stage.

We count ourselves richer for knowing Phyllis. Partnering with her in this vocation of lifting words on the page and stage is our great joy. Our future ventures with Phyllis will no doubt be a source of adventure, challenge, and leaps of faith wherever the words take us. *Deo volente!*

PART
II

PHYLLIS'S CHALLENGES TO MAINLINE, EVANGELICAL, AND EMERGENCE CHRISTIANS

FOUR

LIFE ON THE BRIDGE

Stirring Mutual Transformation in the Anglican Institution and the Emergent Frontier

Stephanie Spellers

I was born and raised in Antioch, but I also make my home in Jerusalem. You could call me a dual citizen.

It was in 2007 when I first heard Phyllis Tickle share the tale of these two ancient cities, Jerusalem and Antioch. She was quoting from *An Emergent Theology for Emerging Churches*, where Ray Anderson first drew the symbiotic link between Jerusalem—symbolic seat of powers and institution—and Antioch—that marginal incubator for fresh expressions and mission.[32] Anderson made the case, but it sounded different coming from this steel-haired, sassy-talking, white Southern grandmother, speaking to her peers at the St. Paul Episcopal Cathedral in Boston. Phyllis

32. Ray Sherman Anderson, *An Emergent Theology for Emerging Churches* (Carol Stream, IL: IVP Books, 2004).

took her seat in Jerusalem, and proceeded to draw diagrams and tell stories of emergence and to inform the powers that their future is somewhere over that hill, tied to Antioch.

In those days, her words were manna for Antiochenes in the Episcopal Church. We were margin-riders drawn to something grounded and beautiful in Jerusalem. Thanks to Phyllis, we knew someone with clout—or at least a head full of gray hair—had our backs and shared our passion. Looking at this woman on the bridge, one arm stretched toward Antioch and the other into Jerusalem, we got courage to keep crossing over.

Those crossings got more regular and more mutual: Jerusalem elders making pilgrimage into Antioch; Antiochene emergents traveling into Jerusalem. Now there are more of us bicultural or "hyphenated" leaders, arms stretched into both the mainline church and emergence communities we serve and love, blending the best impulses from each for the sake of God's kingdom.

I know this life because now I live on the bridge between Antioch and Jerusalem. After seven years midwifing an emergence congregation at the Episcopal cathedral in Boston, I recently moved to New York to serve as a canon on the senior staff of the bishop of Long Island. That means I manage missioners and facilitate the engagement of 146 churches with emerging mission contexts in Brooklyn, Queens, and the whole of Long Island. Across the East River in Manhattan is the Episcopal Church headquarters. At special services I wear a formal black cassock with crimson piping, a mark of stature and proximity to power. Make no mistake: this is Jerusalem.

Yet Antioch is never far away. As a black female priest under forty-five who planted a church made up of mostly twenty- and thirty-somethings, half of them lesbian, gay, bisexual, or transgender, I have a heart for Antioch. My tiny studio apartment is in Brooklyn; each day I walk outside and see Antioch, a diverse land where the institutional church's powers hold little sway. Here, the margins are central. I am grateful for that reminder. If I forget them—if I forget Antioch—I am lost.

I was born and raised in Antioch, and it is in my blood. It is where I go to bed and where I wake up. But I hop on a train most days and ride into the heart of the institution, to my seat in Jerusalem. Call me a dual citizen. Call me a "Hyphenated." The more I see of both cities, the more certain I am that our future is together. Antioch needs Jerusalem, and Jerusalem definitely needs Antioch.

WELCOME TO JERUSALEM

Clearly, emergence Christians have long been fascinated with the beauty and mystery, ordered prayer life, spiritual practice, and theological flexibility that find full expression in Anglicanism. Robert Webber charted the path in 1985 with his classic *Evangelicals on the Canterbury Trail*.[33] Since then, Phyllis Tickle has taken up the mantle of ambassador from the Episcopal Church into the emergence frontier, extending a hand to emergence Christians outside of liturgical

---

33. Robert Webber, *Evangelicals on the Canterbury Trail: Why Evangelicals Are Attracted to the Liturgical Church* (Harrisburg, PA: Morehouse Publishing, 1985).

traditions and welcoming them to dig around in our ancient treasure box. For Robert Webber and Phyllis alike, it has been the most natural alliance imaginable. As she has stated,

> Anglicanism . . . holds, with the greatest impunity, the treasures of the church's past. Rome is still too hierarchical. Protestantism is, in a sense, the thing from which Emergent Christians are fleeing. Orthodoxy is still too outré or unfamiliar in Europe and the Americas. Only Anglicanism can claim both a fairly neutral (for Emergences, anyway) history and a more or less direct or unbroken line with early forms and expressions of latinized Christianity.[34]

My daily life bears this truth out. I have been privileged to welcome yearning evangelicals, fallen Catholics, and jaded agnostics to venture from Antioch into the tradition that is, for me, the only one I could call home. But the bridge crossings move both ways. Speaking from within the Episcopal fold, I am aware that the Episcopal future depends on a relationship with emergence, missional Christians.

This would not be news to Phyllis. She has long recognized the bridge dwellers—or Hyphenateds—as pivotal figures in the Great Emergence.

> Hyphenateds are conduits, and conduits, by definition, flow in two directions. While they may be carrying the ancient, the tried, and the exquisitely honed into Emergence

---

34. Phyllis Tickle, *Emergence Christianity: What It Is, Where It Is Going and Why It Matters* (Grand Rapids, MI: Baker Books, 2012), e-book 940.

thought, they are also infusing into their natal traditions the sensibilities, contextualized theology, and reinvigorated praxis of the Emergence Christian community that they likewise refuse to leave.[35]

In other words, Antioch has much to gain from relationship with Jerusalem, and Jerusalem also needs relationship with Antioch in order to be whole. Established, historic churches need Hyphenateds and other bridge figures who will reinvigorate, reframe, and contextualize ancient traditions.

This is especially true for the Episcopal Church. My home church happens to also be the historic home of the slaveholders, the industrialists, the owning class, the managing class, and the Frozen Chosen (sorry, Presbyterians, but when it comes to privilege here on earth, statistics prove that the title belongs to the Episcopalians[36]). As Antiochenes enter and make our claim on the institutions and heritage of Jerusalem, we can serve as loving, insistent prophets who remind a comfortable, established church of its calling and God's mission.

SEEING JERUSALEM FOR WHAT IT IS

That unveiling is a genuine gift, and I hope more and more emergence Christians bear it into the Episcopal Church. For instance, an Episcopal friend recently explained to me that our church has no common theology, which is why we need common

---

35. Ibid., e-book 1,863.
36. See the Pew Forum's U.S. Religious Landscape Survey, which demonstrates that the Episcopal Church has the highest proportion of members who have done graduate study and earn more than $100,000 a year (http://religions.pewforum.org).

prayer (read: if we stray from a strict application of the Prayer Book liturgies, we cease to be Anglican). I was in shock, because Anglican theology is one of the most compelling elements of the whole tradition, and the major reason why I joined the church in 2000—indeed, the Book of Common Prayer is rife with theology. Dual citizens and prophets are necessary to recall the unique theological perspective and gifts on which our prayer and life are founded.

What might the Episcopal Church become if we gazed at ourselves through emergence eyes? If we fully welcomed the partnership between Antioch and Jerusalem, what gifts would come to the fore? At its best and truest, the Episcopal Church is:

Contextual and missional: A primary given for those of us shaped by Antioch and emergence Christianity is context. Anglicans, true to our roots, could not agree more. In 1563, long before anyone coined the term *contextual theology*, the Church of England declared, "It is a thing plainly repugnant to the Word of God, and the custom of the Primitive Church, to have public Prayer in the Church, or to minister the Sacraments in a tongue not understanded of the people."[37] At the time they were arguing against forcing English speakers to pray in Latin. Today, they might advocate for translating our linguistic, visual, and cultural language to embrace Jamaicans in Queens or young adults in Brooklyn's

37. Article 24, Thirty-Nine Articles of Religion, Book of Common Prayer, 872. Note that the Articles in the 1979 Book of Common Prayer were adopted by the American church in 1801. The original thirty-nine articles were originally agreed upon by the Church of England in 1563.

Bushwick neighborhood. For Episcopalians, sharing the gospel means nothing unless you share it in the language of the people.

Reforming yet ancient-affirming: The other Anglican given is the *via media* (middle road): a posture that is at once open to change and new perspectives, but not so open that you quickly swing away from truths established for the ages. We "keep the mean between the two extremes, of too much stiffness in refusing, and of too much easiness in admitting any variation from it."[38] Change for its own sake has little appeal. Standing in the way of change, as a rule, is equally un-Anglican. As Phyllis understands so well, emergence Christians can help us to remember this balance, since they also love ancient enough to usher it into the future.

Benedictine and practice-focused: Whether it is *lectio divina* (meditative, "divine" reading) or the Daily Office (the monastic tradition of ordered, daily prayer on which Phyllis based her books *The Divine Hours*), Episcopalians understand that Christian life may include mountaintop experiences, but it is also a long and beautiful journey fueled by the grace of God and with practices that grow us into the fullness of Christ.

Democratic: Yes, the Episcopal Church has bishops, priests, cathedrals, dioceses, and even a presiding bishop. But this hierarchy is built according to the same pattern, and by the same

38. After St. Augustine, particularly cited in the preface to the Book of Common Prayer..

leaders at the same time, as the American government. That means the system is designed to *never* eclipse the input and voice of the people. Bishops are elected by representatives from each congregation; lead clergy (or rectors) are identified by a church-based search committee; and only a convention made up of laity, clergy, and bishops can make major decisions for the church. If the bishops get out-voted, they accept it and life goes on. It is neither a starfish nor leaderless organization, but it is also a far cry from the authoritarian, Father-Knows-Best systems from which many of us shaped by Antioch and emergence flee.

Incarnational: Emergence Christians know that bodies matter. Jesus's human body mattered, which is why Anglicans have long held the Incarnation next to the Crucifixion and Resurrection as coequal moments in the Christian story. Because Jesus came to join us, in the flesh, human bodies and human experience are not to be cast aside as accidents of a sinful creation. When we say "marvelously made" (Psalm 139) and "made in the image of God" (Genesis 1), we mean it.

Sacramental: One direct consequence of that incarnational theology is a highly sacramental view of the whole creation. Sacraments are "outward and visible signs of an inward and invisible grace": they are the symbols we can touch and see that bear the actual power and presence of Jesus Christ. Communion is a sacrament, as is baptism. But ultimately, for Episcopalians, the whole creation becomes sacramental. Everywhere we look, we have an opportunity to see and touch—and honor—Jesus. Likewise, the scandal of emergence Christianity is its willingness to notice Jesus on the street, in homes, and, yes, in our very bodies.

Inclusive: Because of this high sacramental theology, both emergence Christians and Episcopalians are drawn toward the inclusion and celebration of Christ's life among all people, including the ones driven out of other Christian communities. Consider the final two promises Episcopalians make at baptism, which read like this:

Celebrant (the officiant): Will you seek and serve Christ in all persons, loving your neighbor as yourself?
People (baptized person or sponsor): I will, with God's help.
Celebrant: Will you strive for justice and peace among all people, and respect the dignity of every human being?
People: I will, with God's help.[39]

If you truly believe there is a spark of Jesus in every person, then your Christian life needs to reflect that radical commitment.

Global: To be Episcopalian is to be a Christian in relationship with brothers and sisters, especially those around the globe. We are part of the Anglican Communion, the body of 77 million Christians who hearken back to the Church of England and the Anglican way of being Christian. Every one of those churches is called to be an Anglican expression rooted in its local context, in conversation with partners across the globe. Even the Episcopal Church, the primary branch of the Anglican Communion in

39. Book of Common Prayer, 305.

America, actually includes churches in fifteen other countries in the Americas, Asia, and parts of continental Europe. To be Episcopalian is to be connected and accountable to a much bigger family.

Praying in common: That big family does have such a thing as common prayer. We may pray in different cultural, linguistic, and visual languages, but there is a rhythm of prayer that you can recognize as historic, catholic (with a lowercase *c*, meaning "universal"), and Anglican. That rhythm hums beneath these liturgical movements:

- Welcome the people
- Share the Word of God, including the gospel
- Proclaim the good news, as revealed in the Word of God
- Offer prayers as a community
- Share the Peace of Christ
- Offer our lives and resources back to God
- Gather at the table for Eucharist (or Communion or the Great Thanksgiving)
- Tell the story of Jesus's table fellowship with his friends, and bless, break, and share bread and wine
- Give thanks and praise
- Go in peace to love and serve God

Passionate for liturgy: When most people think of Anglicanism, they think of our passion for liturgy, which rises from a conviction that God seeks particular moments and locations to come, dwell among us, and then carry us to a whole other plane. In liturgy, we truly participate in the divine drama: living, dying, and rising again with Jesus week after week, and slowly growing into grace-filled embodiments of Jesus's life and love in the world. Emergence Christians also tend to be especially attentive to worship and anxious *not* just to go through the motions or do rote prayer by the book. If you ask why, we will say it is because we expect to have a life-changing encounter with God in these moments, and that as a result we will grow a little more like Jesus.

Mystery: How does this transformation into the likeness of Jesus Christ happen? We do not know. At what point in the liturgy or in daily life does the "magic" occur? We could not say. But Jesus has promised that he would draw near. The persistence of this mystery does not diminish our love or faith in Jesus Christ. Rather, faith is a conviction in things unseen (Hebrews 11:1). We do not have to have all the answers spelled out with logical precision to give our lives to God. That is a huge relief to emergence Christians, even as this comfort with paradox places many of us beyond the pale in other Christian communities.

Beauty: Emergence Christians may be comfortable with mystery. If there is one thing about which we are certain, it may be the beauty of holiness and the holiness of beauty. The most compelling theologians of the Anglican tradition are artists, poets, and novelists, from John Donne to George Herbert, C. S. Lewis to Madeleine L'Engle. Even the many scientists and philosophers in our midst—luminaries like Isaac Newton and Charles Darwin—bowed to the beauty of God when logical cognition reached its limit. There are moments on this earth when we can hear angels and see a glimpse of the heavens, and in those moments we know God is in our midst. The only thing to do is to bow . . . and then drop all you have and follow. Or, as Phyllis has observed in the face of such mysteries:

> To ask of a holy and living event that it be confined within the limitations of human comprehension, much less be captured within the fairly recent human concept of historicity, is to violate in every possible way the gift of glimpses that has been given. To reduce it to rules is not just to deny its scope and purposes but also to intentionally obscure and defile its consuming beauty.[40]

THE RESURRECTED BODY OF CHRIST

The Anglicanism that Phyllis and I both love is undeniably emergent, a church that unashamedly claims the shades, beauty, and complexity outlined above. But we are human, and we have faltered. The pressures of empire and establishment have forced us into stagnation. We have often been more invested in creating beautiful structures than in discerning the life of God to which they point. Our hierarchies have become frozen, and we have demanded allegiance to Anglo, upper-class culture as a prerequisite to membership.

40. Tickle, *Emergence Christianity*, e-book, 2,026.

In other words, we have fallen into the Jerusalem trap and gotten caught up in the maintenance of power and institution, instead of participating in the kingdom of God. It is not an unforgivable sin, but we do have to repent. By repent, I mean the ancient concept of *metanoia*—that is, turning or transformation, acknowledging where you were headed and walking in a new way. In relationship with Antioch and emergence Christianity, listening to the witness of leaders like Phyllis Tickle, Episcopalians can walk in reformed yet ancient and beautiful ways.

The first fruits of that reformation have already begun to emerge. I recently traveled from a gathering of Episcopal bishops straight to a gathering of emergence Christians in Memphis, and was shocked to hear similar words peppered throughout both gatherings: *networks, collaboration, wisdom of the margins, movement of the Holy Spirit, emergence and complexity theory, post-colonial church.* Why are bishops engaged in such conversation? It is, at least in part, because they have been in conversation with Antioch.

As I have spoken with Hyphenateds in other denominations, we have been nothing short of awed at the movement's spread. Presbyterians who had resigned themselves to being on the edge of denominational life are now serving on national committees. Lutheran leaders with scrappy, emergent churches are now helping to shape their church's basic approach to mission and ministry. National leaders for the Reformed Church in America are showing up at emergence gatherings and surprising the rest of us with their forward thinking about the structure of the future church.

At the last triennial General Convention of the Episcopal Church, held in the summer of 2012 in Indianapolis, the church's leaders overwhelmingly approved and funded the creation of "Mission Enterprise Zones": areas designated by geography or cultural affinity where local leaders partner with a diocese and the wider church to birth a contextual initiative freed from the more restrictive rules and expectations that control conventional expressions of church. In other words, the Church agreed to invest significant money and to grant new ministries the freedom and permission to follow the lead of the Spirit. Why were church leaders willing to take such risks? Because Antiochenes were at the table, telling our stories, urging partnership and making it clear that we love this church and see it as a vibrant, essential, and relevant community sharing the gospel of Jesus Christ.

The same General Convention also authorized the formation of a group to reimagine the structure of the Episcopal Church and make recommendations for concrete, meaningful transformation before the next General Convention in 2015. Their mandate: imagine for us the shape of a church structured for mission, instead of one where the core mission is perpetuating the church's existing structure. The unmistakable reality is that we have been a church aligned with Jerusalem, but we long for relationship with Antioch, and that means we need different structures, different models, and open spaces to receive the gifts of the Holy Spirit.

Some may see these changes as mere window-dressing. For those of us who have long dwelt in Jerusalem, the transformation is a sign that the kingdom of God has drawn near. Others will point to past renewal movements that showed great promise to transform Jerusalem and then fell short, and see those "failures" as a sign that the greatest hope remains back in Antioch, far from the church's hierarchical, historic power centers. Can Jerusalem change? Can Antiochenes truly make a home in this land and bring Antioch with us?

The truth is, every renewal effort builds on the one that preceded it. Phyllis calls it "peri-emergence": the cracks that precede the total breaking open of emergence. Postcolonial, Latin American, and black liberation theologies made space for feminist theology, which made room for other postmodern and queer theologies, which arose alongside middle-class, young adult–focused movements like the emerging church.

Change like this takes time, or, as a friend recently offered, "Nine pregnant women can't give birth to a baby in one month." This particular change took so much time because of historic firewalls that separated evangelical Christianity from liberation movements. Recall that evangelicalism rose precisely as women, people of color, and LGBT people found greater voice and consciousness. That is no coincidence. Evangelicalism created a cocoon around its adherents, guarding against the "counter-culture" movements shaking the foundations across the rest of America. How would young people raised in these churches have known about liberation theology, contextual theology, or reading the Bible from the underside? They came to this realization the old-fashioned way: by becoming conscious, by asking hard questions and being rejected, and by discovering God on the margins even as they found themselves there.

And so emergence Christianity came to life. A new generation of Antiochenes came knocking on the door of Jerusalem. Now we are here . . . again.

How will we come into the fullness of emergence? How will we grow, as the apostle Paul dreamed it, from glory to glory? It will take the gifts of Jerusalem: historic, beautiful, incarnational, catholic. And it will take the gifts of Antioch: marginal consciousness, curiosity, authenticity. We need the wisdom of those who have lived on the margins allied with those who have cultivated deep knowledge of the ancient ways. And we need dual citizens and bridge dwellers to stretch their arms wide and bring these worlds together.

FIVE

EVANGELICALS ON A JOURNEY TO EMERGENCE

What to Take, What to Leave Behind

Ryan K. Bolger

Through her work on spirituality and emergent forms of culture and faith, Phyllis Tickle has revealed the signs of the times. Beyond creating tools for spiritual practice, she has created a rubric to understand the last 2,000 years of church life through categorization of 500-year epochs of distinctive Christian faith and culture.

The Western Church just completed the epoch of 1500–2000 and the time of Reformation Christianity. Phyllis's grid helps evangelicals see that their experience of the Christian faith is rooted in one particular cultural form—the Reformed one. Now, a global church is entering the time of the Great Emergence, and, as with each epoch, each culture requires a new form of faith to address the deep questions arising from the context.

In this chapter, I explore how evangelicals might benefit from Phyllis's analysis and how evangelicals might prepare themselves for the coming era. Does evangelicalism have a place in this new world of emergence? I assert that evangelicals, because of their ability to prosper apart from institution in an individualized culture, are well suited to serve in the Great Emergence, a cultural paradigm where spirituality without religion is the primary form of faith expression.

REFORMED EVANGELICALS AND INDIVIDUALISM

Western evangelicals look to the Reformation for their roots. They look at Luther's posting of his ninety-five Theses as a model of activism that moves away from institutional faith, focusing instead on the life of the believer before God. The label *evangelical* originally meant anything not Catholic: the Reformers of the sixteenth century were called evangelicals. Generations later, as the new Reformed movements institutionalized and their spiritual vitality waned, evangelicals emerged, calling the faithful through tracts, Bible studies, or open-air preaching, to return to a vital relationship with Christ. Both the Puritan and Pietist movements stressed the need for personal conversion and repentance. Beginning a century later, John and Charles Wesley, Jonathan Edwards, and eventually Charles Finney continued this evangelical pattern of calling the nominally religious to recommit their lives to Christ.

The Reformation was much more than a movement connected to religion, as Phyllis demonstrates in her rubric. The Reformation was part of a larger shift in Western culture, from a mercantile economy to a capitalist one, from fiefdoms to nation-states, from an illiterate populace to a literate one, all giving rise to an educated middle class. Phyllis rightly ties the Reformation to the culture of modernity, to a culture made possible by the printing press. This new culture needed a religion to make sense of its world. She is correct to point out that Christians must be aware that the religious changes in each period were just one part of a larger cultural transformation.

A subtext of modern Reformed culture was the gradual, increased agency of the individual in Western society. Late in the previous epoch, traditional commitments gave way to societal commitments—from the villager to the citizen, from the artisan to the industrial worker, from the clansman to the soldier. Over time in Reformation culture, societal commitments began to lessen as Cartesian, Enlightenment, psychological, and more atomic understandings of the individual developed. Societal controls gave way to the heightened responsibility of the late modern or postmodern individual.

The Protestant Reformation may be seen as a contextualization of the Christian faith into sixteenth-century northern European culture. Evangelicals represented an ongoing renewal movement within Reformation Christianity. Just as Protestantism cannot be understood apart from the rise of modern culture, evangelicalism cannot be understood apart from the rise of the individual in modern society. Evangelicalism is an individualized expression of Reformed faith.

Evangelicals have thrived in the culture of the individual and the values of the Enlightenment. As personal agency increased in the modern period, so did evangelical practice. Religious affiliation might be beneficial but could never substitute for personal repentance, the keystone in the evangelical credo: each person needed to convert to an entirely new way of life. Evangelicals felt the call to individually share their understanding with others, outside the religious institution, in the home or workplace. More than the homily or sermon, it was individual Bible reading that became the primary reference for evangelical life, be it through study or devotional reading. Finally, one's family, community, ethnicity, gender, age, or economic status did not save; for the evangelical, each person comes to Calvary alone.

Throughout their history, evangelicals have initiated a broad range of practices, intentionally outside of institutional controls. Reformation culture provides a space for the widespread practice of individual Bible reading, prayer groups, preaching, revival meetings, accountability groups, mission societies, media ministries such as radio and TV evangelism, and worship music. Eventually, evangelicals created colleges, seminaries, college ministries, and magazines, not to mention new churches, submovements, and political lobbies. Most of these efforts were created outside the jurisdiction of existing power structures.

EVANGELICALS TODAY IN THE PARTICIPATORY CULTURE

In the socioeconomic realm, the producer culture that dominated Reformation culture until World War II waned in the 1960s; a consumer-oriented paradigm was initiated in the 1970s.[41] Religion in the West adopted this logic, and ascriptive ties to religion (e.g., a set of activities one inherited from one's parents, like language or culture) ceased in the West. Instead, all religions shared a level playing field, and churches became one of many spiritual options for the seeker to choose. In addition, a plethora of new spiritualities filled the spiritual marketplace. Freed from denominational ties, Christian individuals in a consumer society flocked to the evangelical megachurches of the 1980s. Much more responsive than their traditional forebears, these evangelical institutions created spiritual products and activities designed almost exclusively for individual consumption.

With the birth of the Network Society and the rise of interactive Web practices in the emergence culture of the twenty-first century, Western culture shifted once again, this time from a consumer paradigm to a participatory one. Participatory culture transforms consumption activities into production activities, as the former consumers become cultural producers, remixing consumed media products into new configurations and products.

Evangelical megachurches, designed for the individual spectator, no longer serve as a compelling option for people in emergence culture—people who self-identify first and foremost as *participants*. Emergent individuals desire to produce, interact,

41. Zygmunt Bauman, *Liquid Modernity* (Cambridge, UK: Polity Press, 2000), 76–80.

reveal, and upload their creations for others to experience. An evangelicalism that focuses on a producer/consumer paradigm simply will not thrive in a participatory/emergence culture. However, religious systems that focus on deep levels of participatory immersion, such as an aesthetic neo-monasticism, will thrive.

Reformation Christianity provided the broader context for the seeds of evangelicalism to be planted within an increasingly individualized culture. But, again and again, these new movements, with their clarion call to individual action, evolved into larger institutions, which eventually impeded the freedoms of the individuals who were part of the organization. In addition, these institutions were no longer perceived as embodying the Reformation values of conversion, activism, the Bible, and the cross. However they evolved, these institutions became candidates for renewal just a generation or two after their founding. The evangelical call for a removal of constraints to individual action and enablement of gospel action would need to be sounded again.

EMERGENCE

As defined by Phyllis, the emergence cultural paradigm has developed over the last 150 years or so, as Reformation culture dimmed. New developments in complexity theory and systems theory signaled the upcoming changes in culture. Emergent citizens prefer dialogue, offer hospitality, think in decolonizing ways, are stridently antiauthoritarian, and refuse hierarchy; they value community, authenticity, and transparency.

Emergent religion is characterized by a focus on deinstitution-alization, community, plurality, social justice, the embrace of material reality, the sacralization of all of life, an embrace of science, and innovative appropriations of tradition.[42]

Emergence culture is not a postindividualist culture: the individual is still a choosing creature free of ascriptive ties. But these individuals are choosing to immerse themselves into a deeply communal and participatory world. It is not an isolated, lonely *me*, but the deeply *connected me* that dwells in this new world of connectedness and participation.[43]

Emergence Christianity, a subset of both emergence culture and religion, began with the Azusa Street Revival in 1906, in Los Angeles, according to Phyllis. Led by uneducated preachers, many barriers were crossed, including racial, economic, age, gender, cultural, and denominational. Just a few years later, when Walter Rauschenbush introduced the Social Gospel, a social justice component was added to the other early characteristics of emergence. With the birth of the Taizé movement in 1943, all the components of an emergence Christianity were displayed: a deeply communal, hospitable, and ecumenical movement dedicated to global peace and justice, all expressed within an incarnational, neomonastic aesthetic. Before the middle of the

42. Ryan K. Bolger and J. Shawn Landres, "Emergent Religion," in *Encyclopedia of Global Religion*, ed. Mark Juergensmeyer and Wade Clark Roof (Thousand Oaks, CA: Sage Publications, 2011), 340–42.
43. Lee Rainie and Barry Wellman, *Networked: The New Operating System* (Cambridge, MA: MIT Press, 2012), 19.

twentieth century, Phyllis asserts, emergence Christianity had revealed its form.

Because of the increased agency of individual in the West, and therefore a deep suspicion of institutions, these movements at the margins of Christianity will become the primary Western expression of faith in the twenty-first century. It does not appear that Christian institutions will dominate in the West as they have in the previous three epochs. As Phyllis makes clear, a deinstitutionalized church, beyond the denomination and even beyond the congregation, seems to be the future of the church.

TOWARD AN EVANGELICAL EMERGENCE

In a Reformation culture, where societal commitments governed how people formed their way of life, evangelicals were the ones who internalized the theological innovations of the Reformation and contextualized those forms into a nascent culture of individualism. In emergence culture, where all citizens are individualized—choosers, free of all ascriptive ties and anti-institutional in disposition—what is the role for evangelical faith? How might evangelicals continue our work in yet another culture where high levels of personal agency abound?

Evangelicals must bring their entrepreneurial skills and inclinations to bear on emergence culture. Through their own initiative, evangelicals pray and read the Bible, share their faith, start small groups, support missionaries, worship at special events, and create messages for new media, be it print, radio, TV, or Internet. Evangelicals cultivate a spiritual network of friends without regard to institutional religion. If emergence is the time for a do-it-yourself spirituality, where one cobbles together a spiritual life from many sources across the network, outside typical church structures, then evangelical dispositions toward an engaged faith will serve them well.

The evangelical has always destabilized church practice—the inner call trumped those activities that seemed to perpetuate the institution rather than personal spirituality. Where evangelicals must tread very lightly, however, is in regard to day-to-day theology and practice in an emergence culture. Evangelicalism is an expression of Reformed faith, a theology developed in the late Middle Ages, centuries before emergence culture. Evangelical theology and practice are responses to questions asked within a previous epoch and culture, but not necessarily answering questions that are being asked today.

Evangelicals must look to the examples of Luther, Calvin, Wesley, and Edwards, not the theologies, practices, and institutions that followed them, for clues about how to engage emergence culture. Beyond the Reformation, renewal agents such as the Desert Fathers and Mothers, the Benedictines, the Franciscans, and the mystics like Teresa of Avila all responded to the culture and faith of their time. Evangelicals, the mystics of the Reformation, created a robust response to the nascent individualistic, middle-class, literate culture of northern Europe. As different as the Desert Fathers and Mothers are from the Puritans or the Wesleys, renewal agents in the coming emergence culture may not appear like the Reformed Evangelicals of the last epoch.

Recognizing that mission always starts from somewhere, how might evangelicals go forward into this new context? Even the best missionaries come to a new culture within the parameters of the sending culture. As much as the missionaries desire to see an indigenous form of Christian faith emerge in the receiving culture, the culturally embedded Christian practices of the missionaries will initially define what Christianity is to the receiving culture. There is no neutral Christianity to offer. To be sure, the goal remains for the new culture to develop a Christian way of life that is characterized by the four "selfs": self-supporting, self-governing, self-propagating, and self-theologizing.[44] But it takes time (and the self-emptying and letting go of the missionaries) to see these faith experiments emerge in the receiving culture.

In their mission to emergence culture, I suggest that evangelicals remember their four marks:

- A commitment to an individually converted way of life
- The Bible as an individual's primary source of authority
- A personal activism that seeks to share their way of life with the world

44. David J. Bosch, *Transforming Mission: Paradigm Shifts in Theology of Mission*, American Society of Missiology Series, no. 16 (Maryknoll, NY: Orbis, 1991), 451–57.

- The cross where each individual receives the life of Christ as mediated through his life and work[45]

Evangelicals must offer these to the emergence culture with open hands, knowing that each of the four will significantly morph as they remix with the receiving culture.[46] For an evangelical-emergent synthesis to occur, the emergent practices of deinstitutionalization, pluralization, social progressivism, and innovation (within tradition) will meet the evangelical marks of conversion, activism, Bible, and the cross. The new synthesis will look different from either evangelicalism or emergence as the two traditions meet and embrace and challenge one another.[47]

CONCLUSION
Possibilities for Evangelical-Emergence

By way of conclusion, allow me to suggest possibilities for evangelical-emergence via the fourfold rubric of evangelicalism.

Conversion

Evangelicals are a people who believe in conversion. Small improvements will not do; one needs to completely redirect his or her life to God. Throughout Reformation culture, the revival

45. Although many definitions might be given, the most widely accepted definition of evangelicalism continues to be David Bebbington's *Evangelicalism in Modern Britain: A History from the 1730s to the 1980s* (London: Unwin Hyman, 1989), 2–17.
46. Those who bring their own tradition into emergence Phyllis calls "hyphenateds." Similar to the evangelical emergent described here, within Christian Protestant circles, there exist Cathomergents, Anglimergents, Luthermergents, Presbymergents, and Baptomergents.
47. This is not new; *evangelical* has been used as a modifier to other traditions. One might be an evangelical Orthodox, an evangelical Catholic, evangelical Anglican, or evangelical Reformed. Richard Mouw describes himself as an evangelical Calvinist (see Mouw, *The Smell of Sawdust: What Evangelicals Can Learn from Their Fundamentalist Heritage* [Grand Rapids, MI: Zondervan, 2000], 71–76).

meeting served to facilitate the conversion of a nominally religious person into a spiritual person. Evangelicals encouraged both adult baptism and personal testimony and downplayed religious affiliation. After conversion, the evangelical convert was to continue in a vibrant faith; if not, they would be considered "lukewarm" or "backslidden," and they would again be a candidate for an altar call. For the evangelical-emergent, ongoing sanctification will be expressed through a dynamic and unceasing practice of spiritual encounter, often expressed in an everyday *rule of life*.

Evangelical-emergents will practice a *material spirituality*. A material spirituality embraces science and its findings in physics and biology, letting go of the long battle against science in regard to cosmic origins and evolution. A material spirituality integrates these findings into a spirituality that sees the connectedness of all things. It welcomes mystery and paradox.

A material spirituality has no hatred of the body. Exercise such as yoga, rest, and a healthy diet all function as spiritual activities. A converted spirituality might practice the seven ancient disciplines as described by Phyllis.[48] A material spirituality remains unapologetically conversionist: all of reality must yield to God and pursue growth to find its full expression.

The spiritual leader is first and foremost a *seasoned spiritual practitioner* (a disciple) before he or she is a leader. He or she must lead from the place of spiritual mastery, regardless of the

---

48. Phyllis Tickle, *Emergence Christianity* (Grand Rapids, MI: Baker Books, 2012), 174.

level of formal education attained. His or her authority comes from serving an exemplary life, one that inspires others; he or she will not prescribe a life for others as much as serve as an example to them. The leaders in these spiritual communities function as spiritual directors more than they do as managers. These leaders may not have had any formal training; education may be a liability, as formal training may lead to more religious expressions of faith. Beyond the spiritual director role, the evangelical-emergent leader may work as a facilitator, creating a space for volunteers to create ministry activities such as worship, small groups, or mission outreach.

Evangelicals have historically been about the heart as well as the head. This need for personal experience and not just a cognitive understanding of the Christian faith will continue in emergence culture. Evangelical-emergents must be spiritual persons on a spiritual journey, headed toward mastery. Their faith practice will be rooted in personal experience, and their spirituality will entail responding to a person—to a God who is calling out to humanity.

Activism

Evangelicals will do well to bring their activism forward into emergence. Evangelicals understand that what they receive in the gospel is not just for them; they have a compelling message that must be communicated to the whole world. Evangelical-emergents will be *apostolic* and will start new ministries as well, and large numbers and longevity will not be a litmus test of success.

Evangelical-emergent affiliations will be guided by *missional action*. Evangelical-emergents will identify with their own groups by sharing in their mission, be it serving, creation care, peacemaking, proclaiming, or justice work. Moreover, they may connect to their group by adopting its rule of life rather than by becoming a member or attending a main church service.

Evangelical-emergents will engage public culture rooted in a deep sense of *equality and mutuality*. They will converse with other traditions, be they within Christianity or within other faiths—or nonfaiths. They will recognize *pluralism* and *mystery* as realities and so they will understand that they see only partially, that ambiguity is a facet of our current reality. As such, evangelical-emergents will approach dialogue with humility.

Bible

Evangelicals, beginning with Luther, have seen the Bible as authoritative, the basis for their faith and practice in everyday life. Evangelical-emergents will see scripture as the overarching *story* of their lives, a story that includes the cosmos, the emergence of life, the peoples of the Earth, and the Hebrew and Christian traditions.

Evangelical-emergents will recognize the *deeply contextual aspects of the Bible* itself and the many ways groups and cultures have appropriated it through history. It will receive the different liturgies, creeds, symbols, rituals, and practices often taken directly from the Bible, or deeply inspired by it, for their worship. So, evangelical-emergents might appropriate Orthodox, Catholic, Protestant, and Pentecostal liturgies as biblical practices immersed in the cultures of their time and place.

Evangelical-emergents will bring forward their stories from the Bible—stories of liberation and redemption. The Bible's context was undeniably different from ours today, and so receiving an agenda for specific political action might be elusive. However, the Bible was not silent on how the community of God was to live in the world. The world beyond the church might be given over to slavery or patriarchy or any number of fallen structures, but the community of God was to live into the coming kingdom, where differences are celebrated and overcome, all are equally valued, and each person has a voice and something to offer. This was a characteristic of the early Christian communities, and it serves as a challenge to the evangelical-emergent today.

The Cross

By taking up one's cross, an evangelical adopts a life of social nonconformity, not for its own sake, but in situations where the powers need to be called to account when they do not conform to the world God is bringing into being. *Taking up one's cross* puts the cross of Christ right at the center of the evangelical-emergent's life.

The orthodox view of the atonement, with Jesus's victory over the powers, thereby making a way for persons to not only bear God's image but to come close to his likeness within Trinitarian relationship, seems compelling within emergence Christianity, and this may work for an evangelical-emergent synthesis going forward. The Eastern Orthodox conception that God became human so that humans could become God is a highly relational, transactional understanding of the Incarnation and the cross that evangelicals may find consistent with their emphasis on the centrality of God's action at Calvary.

The cross invites individuals into a new life of rich abundance, but first they must die. Each one must let go of all that does not coincide with God's ways, receive forgiveness, and he or she must align themselves with God's in-breaking kingdom. It is a personal dying to all the fallen systems of the world and a living into the new reality of Christ. It is a "no" to oppression, marginalization, isolation, and exclusiveness. It is a "yes" to the reign of God and the work of the Holy Spirit in the world.

Phyllis Tickle, most specifically through her work over the last two decades, provided Christians, regardless of their particular tradition, with a road map into emergence culture. I have explored what an evangelical-emergent synthesis might look like, given evangelicalism's long history as a contextualized faith for an individualized culture. I have suggested that evangelicals might come with open hands, offering their vibrant tradition to an emerging context of connection, holism, and participation. Through integrated practices of a converted spirituality, a holistic engagement with world, a wide sense of God's story, and a fresh engagement with the cross, it is hoped that evangelicals might thrive in emergence culture.

SIX

EMERGENCE AS CONVERSATION, NETWORK, AND MOVEMENT

Brian D. McLaren

In the decades since the 1950s and 1960s, several key social movements have reshaped the world: the civil rights, Chicano, and American Indian movements in the United States, the Northern Ireland Civil Rights Association in the United Kingdom, the ecclesial base community movement in Latin America, the antiapartheid and other independence movements in Africa, and the broader student, environmental, feminist, and gay-liberation movements around the world. Thousands of social movement leaders gave birth to these movements, often at great cost.

Behind these social movements were intellectual (or philosophical) movements: postmodernism and deconstruction, postcolonialism, postpatriarchy, postliberalism. And intertwined with these intellectual movements were theological movements, including black theology, liberation theology, feminist theology, eco-theology, process theology, missional theology, and the Social Gospel. In all their swirling complexity, these intellectual and theological movements influenced one another, and they achieved something together in synergy that they couldn't have achieved separately and independently.

If this landscape weren't complex enough, we must also add spiritual movements—shifts, departures, and convergences relating to the lived spiritual and liturgical lives of faithful people, including such diverse and in some ways contradictory phenomena as the charismatic movement, the church growth movement, the seeker movement, the contemplative spirituality movement, the prosperity gospel movement, and the new monastic movement.

Although she hasn't used these four categories explicitly— social, intellectual, theological, and spiritual—Phyllis Tickle has become the leading participant-observer and chronicler-analyst of these diverse and dynamic phenomena, and she has given them a combined name: emergence Christianity. "In very much the same way spring slips up on us week by week every year," she explains, heralded through "a thousand harbingers," this emergence has been gaining ground, and we are finally beginning to acknowledge that it's time to take off our winter coats and dig out the kites, lawn chairs, and flip-flops of spring.[49]

Just as spring pops into view from time to time and place to place—a daffodil here, a robin there, a flock of migrating geese above, greening grass below—emergence Christianity shows up

49. Phyllis Tickle, *The Great Emergence* (Grand Rapids, MI: Baker Books, 2008), 14.

unconvincingly and sporadically at first: a large conference here, small cohorts there, augmented by outdoor festivals, scholarly conversations, and late-night meet-ups in a coffee shop or pub somewhere near a denominational convention. Like spring, emergence Christianity sometimes seems to disappear entirely as a snowstorm signals a resurgence of winter or a warm front suggests an early summer. Because this complex convergence of movements has no real estate or headquarters of its own, no officers or president, no official institutional sponsors, it's easy to ignore, for a while at least. But like spring, it builds momentum and eventually everyone agrees that the regime of winter has lost its grip and there's no going back.

Although it lacks the conventional supports of buildings, budgets, and boards of directors, emergence Christianity does depend heavily on a single technological sponsor: the Internet. All day, every day, countless websites and blogs host interaction and disseminate new questions, insights, and resources. The Web links people with traditional media like books, and it does so in a way that crosses old ethnic and denominational barriers: evangelicals and postevangelicals, charismatics and Eastern Orthodox, Anglicans and traditional Protestants, progressive (pro-Vatican II) Catholics, people from the Peace Church traditions, and others—some quite unexpected—who don't fit neatly in any of these categories.

In her books and lectures, Phyllis Tickle has shown how participants from all these categories are converging and emerging in this nameable phenomenon.

The name "emergence Christianity" may stick. It may not. Either way, Phyllis's uniting of these diverse phenomena under one name is important, I think, for several reasons, among them this: a single name simplifies the past and present so that participants can turn their attention toward the future.

And the future is an open question.

Are the many regional and denominational networks associated with emergence planning to do anything beyond relate and talk? Are they going somewhere? Are they going to converge to do something? Is the emergence conversation becoming a bona fide global movement? Are we ready to make concrete proposals and move in collaboration to see them become a reality? If so, what are our proposals and to whom are they directed? In short, is emergence Christianity the beginning of a new social, intellectual, theological, and spiritual movement, or is it the end result of the movements that have gone before?

A MOVEMENT OR NOT (YET)?[50]

Some of us have been more sluggish than others about using the term *movement* to describe the Great Emergence. We have talked about emergence as a conversation, leading to friendships, which create a relational network. Many thought it would take decades of network-building before there was enough of a groundswell for a movement to occur.

50. Much of the material that follows is also presented in another form in an as-yet unpublished document to which I contributed. It will be available from Mesa, a global expression of emergence Christianity: www.mesa-friends.org.

But within just a few years, what many thought would take decades has come to pass. Space has opened up for new conversation. New churches—and new kinds of churches—are being planted. Waves upon waves of creativity—theological, missional, liturgical, academic—are being unleashed. Institutions are taking notice: some are closing their doors, but others are opening them wide.

But even with all these encouraging signs, those of us who have been hesitant to speak of emergence Christianity as a movement have at least four reasons for our reluctance.

First, some of us felt that if the bus left the station without sufficient gender, racial, ethnic, ecumenical, and socioeconomic diversity on board, the movement wouldn't go very far or accomplish very much. To that end, representatives from various networks have been investing a lot of time in building relationships with a whole range of people, beyond the circle of those who usually are at the center of things in most religious settings. This network diversification was costly for all of us, in terms of time, travel, and sometimes painful conversations as we sought to overcome longstanding patterns of privilege and exclusion. But it was essential and every investment of energy in crossing old boundaries has already been abundantly rewarded.

Closely related to this need for gender, racial, ethnic, ecumenical, and socioeconomic diversity, many of us believed that what was needed wasn't simply a movement in the "the West" where the Christian faith has been in various stages of decline. We needed a truly global movement that spanned East and

West, South and North. We knew from extensive travel and online interactions that parallel movements—part of a global Christian emergence—were springing up around the world. We felt it would be tragic for Americans and Europeans to once again press on as if the rest of the world didn't exist or matter. Nor could they forge ahead with their own plans and then invite others to join them as "tokens" later on. No, there must be true global partnership and shared ownership before the movement was launched.

Third, a number of us felt that some pieces of our puzzle were missing. Largely, those missing pieces were theological. We were rethinking some things, but our intuition told us that we still had a long way to go. It wouldn't be wise to move forward—movement style—until "the fullness of time" when we reached some sort of theological tipping point, when the new paradigm not only solved critical problems in the old paradigm, but also was rich enough to inspire even greater commitment, worship, joy, justice, and peace.

Finally, some of us knew that effective movements make clear, bold, and far-reaching demands or proposals. For several years, we had been (appropriately) focused on raising new questions, not making movement-galvanizing proposals or demands. We knew that our questions could, over time, naturally lead to new understandings, and those new understandings could eventually lead us to make proposals or demands. But we felt that until we were ready to make those clear and bold proposals, we should understand ourselves to be a conversation and a network, a movement in gestation perhaps, but not yet a full-fledged movement.

Now, we have greater gender, racial, theological, cultural, and global diversity at the table. We have crossed a threshold so that our theological questions are beginning to yield new, fertile, substantial, and coherent theological understandings. We are at the point of articulating proposals or demands, and so the Christian Emergence Movement (or whatever it should be called) may indeed be coming to its kairos moment now. For that reason, we need a better theology of movements, institutions, and communities.

A THEOLOGY OF MOVEMENTS, INSTITUTIONS, AND COMMUNITIES

A lot of us have accepted a narrative that says institutions are bad and movements and communities are good. But it's becoming clear that the problem isn't institutions, it's institutionalism. So we are starting to think about institutions, movements, and communities in new and synergizing ways:

1. A community is a human organization connected to the same land or ecosystem.

2. An institution is a human organization that serves its community by preserving the gains made by past movements.

3. A movement is a human organization that serves its community by proposing gains to current institutions.

4. A movement has two paths to success. First, it can succeed when an institution embraces its proposals. Or, if the institution refuses its proposals, it can form a new institution to embody and preserve them.

5. Once institutions accept the proposals of a movement, that movement has no reason to exist, unless it then creates new proposals to offer, and in a sense becomes a new movement, or a new chapter or phase of the ongoing movement.

6. Of course, if a movement forms a new institution to embody its proposals, that new institution can be depended on to resist the next movement that comes along proposing new gains. Why? Because it isn't easy to conserve the ever-growing bank of wisdom, practices, values, protocols, laws, habits, and so on that it exists to conserve.

7. Both institutions and movements are organized, though differently and with different purposes. Both institutions and movements work with power. Both find one another problematic. And each, in the long run, needs the other.

8. When our institutions devolve into bureaucracy and institutionalism, trading their original purpose for the comfort or regime-continuation of the elites who run them and derive the most benefit from them, we depend on movements to challenge, refocus, reform, and revitalize them, and when necessary, to create new institutions as an alternative to them.

9. Movements and institutions are important for everyone, but most people don't build their lives around them. Their lives are lived in communities that are sometimes supported and sometimes harmed—often invisibly or unconsciously —by their institutions and movements. As Slavoj Žižek has written, "The success of a revolution [or movement] should not be measured by the sublime awe of its ecstatic moments,

but by the changes the big Event leaves at the level of the everyday, the day after the insurrection."[51] So neither movements nor institutions are, in the end, the point: robust communities are, where conviviality and creativity thrive as reflections of our living, creative God.

10. The Holy Spirit works in and through movements, institutions, and communities. All are important in the *missio Dei.*

With these insights in mind, we can look back and see how we have been prepared for this moment, and then we can look forward to anticipate what's next.

A BRIEF HISTORY OF MOVEMENT DEVELOPMENT

American thinker Parker Palmer proposes that movements are born in four predictable phases, and his schema describes our experience very well.[52]

1. Divided No More

Isolated individuals experience an incongruity between what the dominant institutions tell them they should say, think, feel, and do and what they honestly believe they should say, think, feel, and do. As this internal division between institutional norms and internal integrity grows, these isolated individuals may remain outwardly loyal, but they gradually lose confidence in the logic of their institutions. As a result, they also lose their fear of

---

51. Slavoj Žižek, *First as Tragedy, Then as Farce* (London: Verson, 2009), 154.
52. See http://www.couragerenewal.org/parker/writings/divided-no-more, accessed November 1, 2013.

institutional punishments, realizing that "no punishment anyone might lay on us could possibly be greater than the punishment we lay on ourselves by conspiring in our own diminishment."[53] So they begin to speak out.

2. Communities of Congruence

As isolated individuals lose their fear and develop the courage to differ graciously, they start speaking up, and as a result, they find one another. They create "autonomous zones" where they can think and speak more freely. They practice operating by new sets of social rules. Participants feel safe, sane, and honest in these cohorts, and their fragile new convictions take shape and strengthen until they are ready to speak them more openly in the public realm.

3. Going Public

When they gain sufficient confidence in private forums, these communities begin to speak out in public, defying institutional norms, articulating new visions, often developing new language and even new paradigms for the future. They express their differences with institutional norms as grievances, demands, refusals to comply, and proposals for change. They gain critics who do them the essential favor of scrutinizing their proposals, challenging them to temper or improve those proposals, or abandon them. Converts are gained, leaders emerge, and the movement is born.

---

53. Parker Palmer, *Healing the Heart of Democracy* (Hoboken, NJ: John Wiley and Sons, 2011), 185–86.

4. *Alternative Rewards*

When challenged by movements, institutions withhold their rewards from movement participants, and often they impose punishments as well: marginalization, stigmatization, expulsion, even persecution, imprisonment, and execution in some cases. In response, movements must create alternative reward systems, thus relativizing the sanctions by which institutions maintain power. They compensate for the withheld institutional rewards by providing their own rewards, some external (jobs, income, status, visibility, colleagues) and some internal (excitement, vision, hope, moral urgency, belonging). Beneath all of these rewards, though, one essential reward sustains them: the relief of living "divided no more." Eventually, the emerging logic of the movement may alter the longstanding logic of the institution(s) from which the movement emerged.

Around the world, although concrete proposals were not being articulated in any kind of unified, self-conscious way, unspoken proposals were taking shape. At first, they were quite modest and limited to the realm of praxis: *We need to bring together some young Christian leaders to reimagine church for the future, because it isn't working so well for our generation.*

Often, more radical proposals followed: *In light of the profound shifts occurring in our culture, we need to reimagine more than how we "do church"—we need to grapple with deeper questions about our theology, starting with God and gospel.*

Predictably, these more radical conversations drew more intense criticism, and some decided it wasn't worth it to challenge existing norms any further. But others were attracted to these deepening proposals, and new support began to arise from a number of institutions: publishers, seminaries, denominational groups, conference and event planners, and more. Although none of these initiatives ever attracted much in the way of actual money, amazing amounts of talent and energy flowed into these proposals to explore theological terra nova together.

Soon it was clear that our theological foment would not stop in the realm of belief and theory. Theological rethinking would lead to a rethinking of many if not all areas of Christian faith, formation, life, action, and mission. Increasing numbers of Christian leaders around the world realized more fully the degree to which we all were in the midst of a paradigm shift, a "great emergence." By the middle of the last decade, they shared an unspoken proposal that could have been articulated like this: *In light of our ongoing theological reflections and reformulations, we need to connect a wide range of Christian leaders to reimagine liturgy, mission, social justice, spiritual formation, leadership development, authority, church structures and connectionalism, interfaith relationships, and more.*

While all this was happening within the Christian community, important conversations began with rabbis who saw themselves as "the Jewish Emergent." Similar conversations have begun with self-confessed emergent Mormons, Muslims, and others. They wanted to talk with us, and we with them, so that together we can share what we are learning and perhaps find ways to work together for the common good.

SIGNS OF AUTUMN OR SPRING?

Although Phyllis heralds these developments as signs of spring, other observers are less hopeful. *No, these are signs of autumnal decline, decay, and disintegration,* some say. *Better days are behind us, not ahead.*

No, sadly, winter is here to stay, others argue. *So we might as well hunker down and get used to it.*

Some are ambivalent: *Yes, Phyllis is right about emergence, but it's not Phyllis's version that is emerging; it's ours!*

Is Phyllis premature to proclaim good news of joy and hope? Or are her critics too invested in past or present to seize an emerging future? Time, of course, will tell. But time will not tell by current realities "hardening" and setting in for the long haul. That is the nature neither of spring nor of emergence Christianity. What emergence Christianity can or will become has not yet appeared. It is not a predetermined, inevitable reality to which people must adjust. It could easily stumble, crumble, and fail to fulfill its potential. It is something waiting to be created, not merely predicted.

In that way, perhaps it is less like spring, whose coming (and passing) is inevitable, and more like a farm in spring, whose harvest is not guaranteed.

The coming of spring is certainly necessary for a farm to thrive for another year. But if the farmers don't get out and work—plowing soil, planting seeds, mending fences, tending weeds—this year will end with the farm in bankruptcy.

With that in mind, if we agree with Phyllis that the season has turned and that something fresh and new is in the air, then, yes, let's take off our shoes and enjoy the feel of greening grass and warming ground for a day or two. But then, we had better put on our work boots and blue jeans. We'd better reach for our rakes and shovels and seed-bags and pruning shears. We'd better get ready for dirty hands, sweaty brows, and aching muscles as discernment makes way for movement.

In this way, Phyllis's proclamation of good news is also an invitation to good work, in the hope of a good harvest. Such is the mission of an evangelist of the future.

PART
III

PHYLLIS'S LEGACY AS MIDWIFE, FRIEND, AND PRAY-ER

SEVEN

MOTHERING AN AUTHOR THROUGH THE BIRTH OF A BOOK

Phyllis Tickle as Doula

Sybil MacBeth

MOTHERHOOD AND DOULAS

My first doula was a woman named Nancy. At twenty-eight years old I was determined to experience pregnancy, birth, and motherhood *my* way. In preparation for the birth of our first child, I read every available book on natural childbirth and breastfeeding. And, except for an unexpected labor-inducing drug called Pitocin and bouts of back pain, labor and delivery met my expectations—no anesthesia, a Lamaze birth, husband Andy in the labor room with me, and a beautiful son named Adam.

Three days postpartum, the victory of a successful birthing experience vanished. I was on my own and attempting to breastfeed. I knew all of the rules about nursing a baby, but I had never been on the playing field with breast and baby in tow. Reading the play manual had not prepared me for sore nipples, a screaming baby at 3 AM, the time and energy required to fulfill the endless demand for milk, and the lack of sleep (mine and my baby's).

My support system included Andy and two nervous grandmothers. Neither of the grandmothers had nursed their babies, and both were certain of Adam's impending starvation, encouraging me to stop breastfeeding and feed him with a bottle and formula. I needed help and support, but not the anxious and critical advice of relatives.

In desperation I called the only experienced woman I knew in town. Nancy was a mother of three, an Episcopal priest's wife, and a certified La Leche League leader (the organization of breastfeeding mothers). Those descriptors qualified her to walk with me into the tangled briars and thickets of parenting and to mother me into motherhood. She taught me the techniques of breastfeeding, answered my desperate phone calls day and night, spoke calming words to me when I knew I could not survive another minute, and introduced me to a community of women who supported each other in the daunting tasks of nursing and mothering. Nancy became my doula, a woman who mothers a mother during pregnancy, birth, and the early days of motherhood.

Dana Raphael may have been the first person to use the Greek word *doula* in its contemporary form, back in 1966. In her book *The Tender Gift: Breastfeeding*, Raphael defines *doulas* as "those individuals who surround, interact with, and aid the mother at any time within the perinatal period which includes pregnancy, birth, and lactation."[54] In various cultures, the role of the doula differs somewhat, but the important fact is "she is *there*. Her very presence gives the mother a better chance of remaining calm and nursing her baby."[55] Because she was a skilled outsider, Nancy did for me what my fearful and emotionally involved relatives and husband could not. She gave me information, confidence, and encouragement.

ANOTHER KIND OF DOULA

Almost thirty years later, Phyllis Tickle became another kind of doula for me. She mothered me into the ego-boosting and ego-busting world of religious writing. She helped me through the labor and birth of my first book.

I first met Phyllis two months before 9/11. She was the keynoter at a Christian education conference at Shrine Mont in Orkney Springs, Virginia, entitled, "Spirituality in the 21st Century." During her plenary sessions Phyllis took the whole room on a journey of history, spirituality, science, physics, and sociology. Through narrative and storytelling chronicles we heard a memoir of our church family—relatives from the past and those just being

---

54. Dana Raphael, *The Tender Gift: Breastfeeding* (New York: Schocken Books, 1973), 24.
55. Ibid.

born—with all of its dysfunctions and familial clashes. I took copious notes in my black marble Mead composition book; she barely used a note. She was brilliant and articulate, funny and insightful.

Breakout workshops and sessions led by Phyllis followed her keynote addresses. They did not interest me. One was a workshop called "Writing for the Religion Market." Why would I need that? I was a full-time community college math professor. I had no illusions of having something to say in the arena of spirituality and religion.

Phyllis also convened people to "pray the hours" three times a day using her newly published *The Divine Hours.*[56] It was that book's first birthday. As usual, I was struggling with prayer, but praying the hours felt like just more words—another Book of Common Prayer. In my personal prayer life, I struggled to sit still, to pay attention, to find the right words for my prayers. I hated my own ineloquent prayer words, but I was tired of everyone else's, too. I had been a pray-er since I was just a tot, but not a very good one; I had prayed in a dozen different ways with only short-term success. *The Divine Hours* would not work for me, I was convinced, but one thing was clear: Phyllis was a woman who was serious about her prayer life. And about prayer, period.

The marble notebook in which I took notes from Phyllis's talks was also my personal journal, the place I noted my frustrations, brainstorms, and ideas. On the third day of the conference I wrote,

---

56. Phyllis Tickle, *The Divine Hours: Prayers for Summertime—A Manual for Prayer* (New York: Doubleday, 2000).

"I wish Christian prayer had more embodiness." Embodiness is not even a word, but I knew what I meant—less head, fewer words, less sitting in a chair with feet on the ground and hands folded.

After the conference, I purchased and read Phyllis's memoir, *The Shaping of a Life: A Spiritual Landscape.*[57] Maybe her prayer form wouldn't work for me, but she was a kindred spirit. One of her favorite activities was also mine—she liked to go to bars alone and hang out there with a good book.

In 2002, about seven or eight of my friends and family members were diagnosed with an assortment of awful cancers—brain, breast, skin, blood, and lung. I prayed puny words of intercession for them—pleas for healing, for comfort, for a few more years of life. My prayers felt silly and small compared to the magnitude of their diseases.

One morning, after a spring semester of teaching math ended, I grabbed a basket of colored markers, pens, and paper and headed to the screened-in back porch. I am not an artist, but doodling with the tools of an artist helps me to leave the left-brained world of equations and formulas and jump hemispheres to my more playful right brain.

I drew an amoeba-like shape and added lines, arcs, squiggles, and color. Without any conscious thought, I wrote the name *Sue* in the middle of the shape. Sue, my sister-in-law and the mother of two school-age kids, had stage-four lung cancer. After five or

57. Phyllis Tickle, *The Shaping of a Life: A Spiritual Landscape* (New York: Doubleday, 2001).

ten minutes of drawing and focusing on Sue's name, I realized I was praying for her without words. Drawing kept my eyes, hands, and mind engaged, while I became quiet and listened, offering Sue into God's care.

This wordless way of praying, which I called "praying in color," became my main form of intercessory prayer, the way I prayed for all of the people on my prayer list. It also became my listening prayer, the way I quieted the noise in my mind and became still enough to pay attention to God. I didn't tell anyone for a long time. My husband became my first confidant. After six months, I told another friend. It seemed like a weird way to pray, maybe even religiously illegal.

In late 2003, Andy and I were exploring the possibility of moving to Memphis, Tennessee. Andy was one of the candidates for the position of senior pastor/rector of a downtown Episcopal church. Phyllis, I remembered, was from somewhere in Tennessee. I found her website, wrote an email asking if she knew anything about Memphis and the church, and pushed the Send button with my inquiries.[58] Her response was immediate and long! She wrote about Boss Crump and the history of Memphis, her farm north of Memphis in a town called Lucy, as well as her close relationship to the particular Episcopal church we were soon visiting.

Andy got the job and we moved to Memphis in February 2004. A month after the move, Phyllis invited me to eat lunch at the Women's Exchange—an 1885 Memphis nonprofit with a tea

---

58. Unless noted, this and all subsequent quotes from Phyllis Tickle are from private email correspondence to Sybil MacBeth from 2004 to 2005. Used with permission.

room and a shop where women have sold their beautiful handiwork and children's clothing for almost 130 years. It seemed an apt choice by the woman who had filled me in on Memphis's rich and checkered history. We got to know each other over ladies' lunch food.

On a whim I had brought one of my marble-composition note-books filled with journal entries, notes from conferences, daily writing, and more recently, pages of my doodled prayers. By the time we moved to Memphis I had been praying in color for about a year. I thought Phyllis might be interested since the seed for this way of prayer came at the conference where I had met her two and a half years before, and had envied her way of praying with words but wished for a way to pray without them. Although it was a very different way of praying from *The Divine Hours*, I really had no fear of her disapproval or rejection.

She paged through the notebook of prayers and said, "You're going to write a book on this." Being in awe of most anything she said, I responded, "Yes, ma'am." What else does a good Southern woman (well, not so good or so Southern) say to Phyllis Tickle?

I went home and immediately started to write. I wrote about growing up as a Christian Scientist, about getting C's in art and being ashamed, about making art through designing and sewing my own clothes, about loving color, about praying. Within days of our first lunch together, I sent my first paragraphs to Phyllis, wondering whether the invitation to write had just been some polite Southern thing. I waited for her approval—or an apologetic retraction of her permission slip for me to write.

Her first response was something like "Why haven't you been writing? Keep it coming." It was just enough encouragement to send me back to the computer. With her first email to me, Phyllis became my doula. She became the person who urged me on in the pregnancy, labor, and delivery of my book. Like a good doula, she was *there,* helping me to stay calm in this new birth experience. In the arena of writing, I was an "aging primipara"—a woman over thirty giving birth to her first child—and I needed all the support I could get.

Sybil-droppings landed in Phyllis's in-box at least once a week. I held my breath while I waited to hear from her. Her responses were quick, usually by the end of the day. The quick responses were often moments of delight for me: "This is wonderful! Droll, self-deprecating, funny, and very, very enlightening and instructive. Do NOT stop! ....p" Like the doula at a childbirth, she was cheerleading, urging me on, one breath, one sentence, at a time.

When the response time was longer than a day, it meant she was thinking. The delayed return email often came with words like these: "I don't get this. The idea was very, very clear without the added words." She never edited ("Editing will come later," she said), but in those thoughtful responses she redirected and guided me to my own process of self-editing. Her comments felt like words of ease, safety, and relief for the writing process, not criticism.

Writing a book and birthing a baby may not be a direct one-to-one correspondence at all stages of the process, but there are some similarities. The "transition" stage of labor, when the body undergoes the radical changes in the uterus and cervix and the hard work of birthing a baby intensifies, was reproduced in the writing process. Transition is often accompanied by nausea, anger, blame, self-doubt, and the desire to run. Many a woman at this stage of labor says, "Whose idea was this? I quit. I've changed my mind. I don't want to be a mother."

I wrote to Phyllis about experiencing all of these feelings sitting at my desk in the midst of the labor and birth of *Praying in Color: Drawing a New Path to God.*[59] I wondered if I had any business writing, if I had anything to say, if this wasn't the stupidest prayer form ever. More than once I wrote, "This feels like self-focused drivel." Like the doula with a mother, Phyllis responded to my needs for immediate assistance and attitude intervention. "It's supposed to. It's called 'the imposter syndrome' and is the most infamous and ubiquitous illness of all those that afflict writers... story that's as old as the profession, Kiddo. Just turn around and snarl at it. You have editors to tell you when it's bad, but never trust your own sense of things. Trust me, this is good crap....p"

Phyllis reiterated her encouragement in response to an encore of my self-doubt: "The emotions you are feeling are well-known territory in writing....I also think that without them or absent their affliction, there is no really good writing...or maybe that's the way I console myself when the beast has got me in its grip."

The generosity and focused attention Phyllis lavished on me was nothing less than my lifeline. I felt safe with Phyllis. Unlike emotionally involved friends and family members, I trusted her

---

59. Sybil MacBeth, *Praying in Color: Drawing a New Path to God* (Orleans, MA: Paraclete Press, 2007).

to be honest with me. This is the role of the doula—to be a calm, nonanxious presence during a potentially painful, fearful, and emotional time. "The *doula* gives a level of support different from that of a person who is intimately related to the woman in labor."[60] "During the process she [the mother] begins to feel confidence in herself and the naturalness of the process."[61] Phyllis reduced my fear factor by many percentage points and helped me to rely on my own abilities.

Brian McLaren, author of numerous books including *Generous Orthodoxy*, has also experienced doula-like care from Phyllis.[62] His writing captivated the wider world of the church, but enraged some of his own church family. "The first time I met Phyllis in person, I was in the middle of getting beat up pretty badly in the Evangelical world. Phyllis gave me a big hug and said something like this: 'My daddy used to say that you can tell a man's character by the enemies he keeps, and judging by yours, I'd say you're a man of sterling character.' Mothered—in the best way possible— is exactly what I felt from Phyllis at that moment: validated, encouraged, and empathized with—without being coddled. That's what I've felt in her presence ever since."[63]

60. Marshall H. Klaus, M.D., John H. Kennell, M.D., and Phyllis H. Klaus, C.S.W., M.F.T., *The Doula Book: How a Trained Labor Companion Can Help You Have a Shorter, Easier, and Healthier Birth*, 2nd ed. (Boston: Perseus Publishing—Da Capo, 2002), 6.

61. Ibid., 18.

62. Brian D. McLaren, *A Generous Orthodoxy: Why I Am a Missional, Evangelical, Post/Protestant, Liberal/Conservative, Mystical/Poetic, Biblical, Charismatic/Contemplative, Fundamentalist/Calvinist, Anabaptist/Anglican, Methodist, Catholic, Green, Incarnational, Depressed-Yet-Hopeful, Emergent, Unfinished CHRISTIAN* (Grand Rapids: Zondervan, 2004).

63. This quote from Brian McLaren is from private email correspondence on June 6, 2013. Used with permission.

The doula does not baby or coddle. Birthing is serious work; it requires courage and stamina. The doula's job is to be gentle but firm. She calms and prods at the same time. A good doula creates an emotionally safe space for the almost-mother to have a shorter, more relaxed birth experience. Phyllis creates such a space for novice and seasoned writers.

Jack Levison, professor of New Testament at Seattle Pacific University, is also no stranger to publication. He has written thousands of pages for articles and books in his field. His scholarly book on the Holy Spirit called *Filled with the Spirit* is 500 pages long.[64] But Jack had a nudge to write a more accessible, popular book on the subject. At the suggestion of a friend, he called Phyllis Tickle for some input. He placed the call on a Friday afternoon with the intent of leaving a message on her phone. Phyllis answered the phone, spent unhurried time in conversation, and invited him to send her examples of his devotionals on the Holy Spirit. "In the midst of packing for a trip the following morning," Jack said, "Phyllis was hospitable, open, expansive, generous, and dear."[65]

In their further communications, Phyllis urged Jack on. "She coaxed me out of the familiar, comfortable womb of academia. Her affirming words about my meditations—'Jack, they're magnificent…brought me to my knees in a place or two'—were

64. John R. Levison, *Filled With the Spirit* (Grand Rapids: Wm. B. Eerdmans Publishing Company, 2009), vii.
65. This and all subsequent quotes from Jack Levison are from phone conversations and private email correspondence from June 9 to June 19, 2013. Used with permission.

gentle forceps drawing my work into the realm of popular religious writing."[66] Phyllis's encouragement gave him the confidence to birth his 2012 book *Fresh Air: The Holy Spirit for an Inspired Life*.[67]

I know dozens of other people who have sent manuscripts to Phyllis for her perusal. With an enormous gift of time and generosity of spirit, she'll read anything sent her way and be completely honest about how she sees the future of the idea and the writing. She does not mollycoddle authors. If she thinks the book has potential, she says so. If not, she is kind but direct, giving her opinion and an explanation for her thoughts. In her farmhouse, a dozen bookshelves containing books with dedications and/or acknowledgments to Phyllis line the walls. (And these are just the ones still left in her house and not archived elsewhere.) These shelves are a nursery of birthed books whose authors in some way experienced Phyllis as doula.

Like any respectful doula, Phyllis helps authors experience their own unique book birth adventure. Phyllis as doula, "an experienced labor companion,"[68] looks on with delight as authors give form and substance to their ideas. Phyllis honored the way I prayed, so different from her own way, and encouraged me to share it. With some lovely irony, I now pray the morning *Divine Hours* online before I do anything else on the computer—and "it works for me."

66. This quote from Phyllis Tickle is from private email correspondence to Jack Levison on August 30, 2010. Used with permission.
67. John R. Levison, *Fresh Air: The Holy Spirit for an Inspired Life* (Orleans, MA: Paraclete Press, 2012).
68. Klaus, Kennell, and Klaus, *Doula Book*, 3.

EIGHT

BOB BARKER, PHYLLIS TICKLE, AND FRIENDSHIP IN THE FUTURE

Doug Pagitt

have a couple of professional heroes. One of them is Bob Barker.

As a kid I grew up with Bob Barker on my television every weekday in the early 1970s. In the early 1990s, Bob kept me company when as a new dad I was the one at home with our kids. There's something perfect about *The Price Is Right* for a parent at home. The show has a cadence that allows you to feel like you are part of the show. The contestants are called out of the studio audience, so even though I was at home I felt like I was a member of the audience—and there was even this little irrational part of me that somehow believed I might be called up. And, when my stated price was the closest to the actual retail price without going over, I yearned for my toddlers to vouch for me when Shelley got home.

Bob Barker was the magical host of that show. With that classy skinny microphone, he would reveal the truth of my guesses. I liked Bob for his wry, almost snarky tone, injected without ever seeming mean to the contestants. But as a viewer I could pick up on the clues—he was a master and somehow made me feel part of it all.

And then there were the rumors of Bob's liaisons with the models on the show (something that made all the sense in the world to me as teenage boy in the 1970s and 80s). And, of course, I was disappointed by the allegations of wrongful termination of some of those models in the 1990s. Nevertheless, Bob Barker seemed to me larger than life—a strange kind of TV star who reminded people at the end of his game show to take care of their animals by having them spayed or neutered. He kept up his mythic TV game show host persona until his retirement in 2007.

But it is none of this makes Bob Barker my hero.

He is my hero because he didn't start hosting *The Price Is Right* until he was forty-nine years old. Let's let that sink in for a moment. Forty-nine years old.

Everything I ever saw Bob Barker do, he did after he was forty-nine. In a world that gives attention and power to the young, the fresh, the new, the unseen, it was stunning to learn that the entire life of Bob Barker, as far as I knew it, came in and after his fifth decade of life.

This has become particularly meaningful as I approach my late forties. Is it possible that my better days are ahead? Is it possible that a person could live a postforties life that has significant meaning for younger generations who are now just six years old? Yes, it is possible, and the likes of Bob Barker illustrate that.

It is with even greater admiration that I think of my other and more significant professional hero, Phyllis Tickle, who even more than being my hero is my role model. Like that famous game show host, Phyllis has made her contribution to my life and the world in her postforties life. If Bob Barker encouraged me to know that it is possible to have a long life in the second half, Phyllis has shown me what that life ought to be like.

I met Phyllis in the early 2000s, first through her books, then her speaking, then through her kindness and friendship. As one of the planners for the Emergent Conventions in 2003, I, along with the other planners, put Phyllis Tickle on our short list of "dream presenters." We hoped that by chance Phyllis would accept our invitation to speak at our event. Little did we know that in the coming years she would not only accept our invitation but would steal the show.

Phyllis was so well received that we structured the final year of the convention around her presentations. In just three years, she had moved from an influence on my life and the emerging movement to a leader and mentor.

I still recall the lunch at that convention where I was asked to approach Phyllis to take what she was presenting and put it in a book as part of a line of books I was coordinating for Baker Books in partnership with Emergent Village. I was really nervous about the meeting. To be honest, Phyllis intimated the socks off me. She was so smart, so tough, so in tune with what was happening in the world of religion that I felt barely worthy of having lunch with her, let alone asking her to turn her esteemed writing career toward the project I was working on.

The moment we sat down to lunch all those fears vanished. Phyllis's warm charm, her quick wit, and her Southern persona made for a great lunch. In fact, as I recall, we had such fun we had to be called back to business by the editor at Baker. We did get down to business, and now several books later that lunch has a lasting legacy.

Over the last nine years, I have come to see that this was not just a connection between the two of us; this is how Phyllis is. She is a friend. She is a friend to all she meets. She, in her life and practice, takes seriously Jesus's call to be friends. I anticipate that Phyllis's legacy will not be only the thirty-six books she has written, the tens of thousands of people she has spoken to, the countless gifts of leadership she has bestowed on hundreds of organizations—I believe that Phyllis will always and firstly be remembered as a friend.

If emergence Christianity is to have as bright a future as Phyllis suggests, then we would do well to not only heed her analysis, but to follow her lead: we should be friends.

This is no simple call. As Phyllis can tell you, and has told me, there are always reasons to put something else before friendship. It is easy to be about strategy or outcomes. It is tempting to distance ourselves from those who are not of benefit to us or who might cause us trouble. But the call of friendship, while not being the easy road, is to be our road.

FRIENDSHIP AS THE EMERGENCE ETHOS

Jesus's call to humanity is extensive. It is a call to personal freedom and structural righteousness. It compels us to care for other people and about God. It beckons us to live the new humanity in loving submission. It is this grand vision that gives such punch to the call Jesus makes to his chosen disciples: "I don't call you servants any longer, because servants don't know what their master is doing. Instead, I call you friends" (John 15:15, CEB). Jesus goes on to finish this thought, saying, "I give you these commandments so that you can love each other."

The agenda of Jesus is intertwined with friendship and love of one another.

Friendship does not come easy for some. Friendship has a dangerous feel to it. It means we are to raise the level of our commitment from tolerance to laying down our lives for one another. When Jesus is quoted as saying, "This is my command-ment: love each other just as I have loved you. No one has greater love than to give up one's life for one's friends. You are my friends if you do what I command you,"[69] we are all implicated.

The notion that we are fulfilling the imagination of God by denominational ecumenism is called into question when we take seriously the idea that we should lay down our lives for

69. John 15:12–14 (CEB).

one another, our friends. We are called to something more than synergy or mutual benefit: we are exhorted to give of ourselves for the survival of the other, even if that means the end of our own dreams and passions.

What would the future look like if each of us from our own tribes and traditions took the idea of being a mutually submissive friend to the other? I have certainly seen this in Phyllis Tickle. Time and again I have seen Phyllis get up early, make airline transfer after transfer, and put her own health at risk in order to sit with people from traditions other than her own, tell them that what they are doing is part of the Great Emergence, and that they should keep going.

We have talked about this and I have asked her how it is possible for her to say yes to almost every invitation, or to write an endorsement for many of the books sent her way (including a number of mine), and she will say something along the lines of, "Oh well, for this person how could I not say yes?" Phyllis takes on everyone she meets as her friend. She begins with friendship as the default. I know she could be more strategic with her time or credibility, but Phyllis will have none of that. She is not interested in being strategic. She wants to be a *friend*.

FRIENDSHIP AND THE FUTURE OF THE CHURCH

In the early years of the 2000s, there were a number of us who banded together to make a generative friendship we called Emergent Village. At the time, we were trying to make not an organization but a relational network of trust and admiration. This was five years before Facebook, when we too used the word *friend* as our primary means of defining our connection.

In *TIME Magazine*'s 2011 profile of him as Person of the Year, Mark Zuckerberg was asked why Facebook succeeded where so many other social networks had failed. He attributed it in part to the fact that Facebook required the user to present their real life and not that of an avatar. And Facebook wanted to be in the business of making people's "real" lives better, not just asking people to endeavor in an alternative "online" life. He said, "In the world, there's trust. I think as humans we fundamentally parse the world through the people and relationships we have around us. So at its core, what we're trying to do is map out all of those trust relationships, which you can call, colloquially, most of the time, friendships."[70]

This is something the emergence Christianity of the future will require: trust. Can we know one another well enough to put ourselves in another's hands? I have seen Phyllis model this so well. Rather than making her own conferences, or creating her own training center, or establishing her own church, she went into other people's places. She was the guest and not the host. She wanted to make their church, diocese, conference, or event the best it could be, and she trusted that these practitioners knew better than her how to put this in practice.

70. Lev Grossman, "Person of the Year 2010: Mark Zuckerberg," *TIME*, Dec. 15, 2010, time.com/time/person-of-the-year-2010 accessed Oct. 23, 2013.

For a well-accomplished person to share ideas and then head home requires a deep trust that others will do something meaningful with what has been shared.

I think there are at least six commitments that can help us live the friendship agenda in emergence Christianity in the spirit of Phyllis Tickle:

1. Make pilgrimage to give one another the gift of our presence.
2. Publicly self-identify with one another.
3. Invite others to participate and welcome new friends.
4. Stay reconciled to one another.
5. Give one another the gift of commitment: not to give up on, betray, or reject one another, but instead, to encourage, honor, and care for one another.
6. Stay informed about one another.

These friendships will need to have both an interpersonal and collective sensibility. There is a need to create the means and vision for collaborative structural sustainability to support and encourage emergence Christianity through a healthy ecosystem for connection among existing and emerging individuals, organizations, and networks.

There is a wonderful opportunity to take advantage of big opportunities with great people who are highly committed to this movement, but there is also a need to move beyond interpersonal networks and personal sacrifice to collaborative structural sustainability. Many of the people Phyllis has met and encouraged in the pursuit of life in the midst of emergence Christianity trust one another and desire to work together for common goals. This collective work will require a new era of innovative leaders and creative risk takers working for long-term partnerships.

These are not easy things to accomplish, but I believe that Phyllis's energy and passion serve as a great inspiration for this collaborative future.

We may not all have the privilege of living into our later years with the vitality of a Bob Barker or Phyllis Tickle, but we are all called to be friends along the way. And we are called to make that friendship sustainable and accessible to all.

So, I will leave you with a blessing that Phyllis has said to me many times: "Be well, my friend."

(Oh, and remember: Help control the pet population. Have your pets spayed or neutered.)

NINE

PRAYER
IS A
PLACE

Reflections on Praying with Phyllis Tickle

Lauren F. Winner

"Thus here are far too many words about prayer these days. It is as if, in our starving, we think a cookbook rather than a meal will feed us. That having been said, there are a few things . . . that I do know about prayer. The first is that prayer is a place." — Phyllis Tickle, *Prayer Is a Place*, p. 68

Phyllis has taught me to pray at least twice over: once in praying with me, and once in creating a breviary that I have used in prayer with other people.

As an Episcopal priest, I am often asked by Christians from other traditions how they might begin a practice of liturgical prayer. The Book of Common Prayer, they say, is a bit daunting, a bit confusing. (Fair enough: it requires lots of flipping around, and many Episcopal churches hand their parishioners worship leaflets on Sunday mornings, so newcomers do not gain comfort with the book itself.) Usually, I send them to *The Divine Hours*. ("The manual strives for simplicity . . . and ease of use," writes Phyllis in the breviary's introduction. "Not only will such an approach reassure those Christians who have not yet begun the practice of keeping the hours, but it will also provide even the liturgically accomplished with what one observer referred to as 'a welcome lack of so many ribbons.'"[71]

I once thought that *The Divine Hours* was a gateway drug for liturgical prayer. But more and more I suspect many people never move on to the Book of Common Prayer or some other prayer book. They might stay forever with Phyllis's breviary.

Most recently, I used *The Divine Hours* in a course I teach at a minimum security women's prison. Half of the students are incarcerated and half are future pastors enrolled at a nearby seminary. The course is called "The History and Practice of Prayer," and each week my friend Sarah and I teach a different prayer practice: first the Daily Office, using a week's worth of prayers from *The Divine Hours*, then Ignatian prayer and *lectio divina*, then doodling prayer, then labyrinth prayer. *The Divine Hours* represents many students' first encounter with praying the psalms, with keeping the hours.

■ ■ ■

71. Phyllis Tickle, *The Divine Hours: Prayers for Autumn and Wintertime* (New York: Random House, 2000), xii.

To pray *The Divine Hours* is, in a way, to pray with Phyllis herself, but I am lucky to pray with her another way, too. Once a month, at an appointed hour on a Saturday, Phyllis and I pray together. We are never in the same place, not on the phone with each other or Skyping, often not even in the same time zone. But we pray together. It is what constitutes friendship, I think.

These shared prayer hours came about some years ago, when, in the midst of divorcing my husband, I heard the Holy Spirit tell me to talk to Phyllis. I suspected she might have some wisdom for me, so I tracked her down, and tracked down her calendar, and got myself to a retreat center where she was staying for a few days, and we sat in her cottage and drank wine and talked. I remember very little of what she said. I remember a few things, but not many things. I remember that I felt lighter when I left.

At the end of our conversation, Phyllis and I went into the gift shop and purchased matching sets of prayer beads—chaplets made by a nun-turned-goat-farmer-turned-prayer-bead-artist (I have heard through the grapevine that she has become a nun again, but I do not know if that is true)—and made this monthly prayer date. Which seems slightly ridiculous in hindsight. I don't keep most other time-bound commitments that I make—to exercise, to write at a certain time each day, even to wake up at a certain time each day. But this one I keep. Phyllis keeps it and I am kept by her keeping.

Phyllis and I never talk about this shared praying. We just pray. I know, because of who she is, that Phyllis is faithful to the prayer. If the actuarial tables are correct, I will outlive her by some decades, but I do not have any question that she will keep these prayer hours with me from heaven.

▪ ▪ ▪

I have been known to pray while walking, or while sitting on a plane, but for the most part, I tend to pray at home, in the house that I have set up just so, with the art that inspires me, with the furniture I adore, down to the favorite fabric of the sofa slipcover.

I have been accustomed for many years to having long stretches of hours alone in my house, and for the most part, I pray when the mood strikes. In the midst of a long day alone at home, I will sometime in the afternoon leave my desk and go to the screened-in porch, or to the living room, and sit in one particular red club chair, or in the oversize and crazily comfortable rocking chair that I inherited from my mother, or sometime I sit on the green sofa. I sit in one of those spaces and pause, luxuriously, in the time alone in this space that I find so very stilling, so conducive. I am usually sitting in the rocking chair when I pray my Phyllis hours. It is quiet, and I am alone, and I pray.

▪ ▪ ▪

In class, at the prison, we are discussing praying the hours. Sarah and I introduced the practice of the Daily Office the week before, and we handed out copies of the date-appropriate pages from Phyllis's breviary, and the week's assignment was to pray the hours each day, and now we are back in the trailer where our class meets, discussing our week of prayer.

Some of our seminary students admit that it was hard to squeeze in all this praying in the midst of their course load, and their part-time jobs, and their boyfriends. It is early in the semester and none of them have learned yet what they will learn—that all of those problems are good problems to have.

The incarcerated women tell us about trying to find, in the prison, space remotely conducive to prayer, especially multiple times a day. There is no space to be alone, no space that is quiet, little time when you are not working or taking a class, little time over which you have even a modicum of control, no time when you can guarantee you won't be interrupted even for ten minutes. There is no time when the intercom will not interrupt, maybe paging you to come get your meds. There is no moment at which you can say, "Now I know I have twenty minutes of peace and quiet."

I cannot imagine praying, never alone; praying, never in quiet. I cannot imagine that. I am so accustomed to my rocker.

I lead lots of spiritual retreats, women's retreats, Lenten Quiet Days, prayer retreats. There is always a discussion of prayer, how hard it is to squeeze it in, how hard among the many demands of children, jobs, the to-do list. All of the advice I dole out at these retreats is useless—illegal or impossible or both—in the prison: light a candle, go to a quiet room, sit in your favorite chair, close the door. Have a special mug for tea and know that mug is your prayer mug; when you settle down with red zinger tea in that mug, you are settling into prayer.

It is not that the incarcerated women can't have any cues that they are entering prayer. It is just that the cues must be more elemental, more stripped down. A certain posture. Perhaps a rosary. Not an open flame or a closed door. The cue is closer to the prayer itself. The praying becomes part of the set-aside space that makes prayer possible.

What I see in the prison is something about the privilege of my own sporadic prayer life. How my complaints about not finding time to pray, my "struggles" to "find time" to pray, are a privilege of the free.

It is perplexing and painful to realize that your devotional life is a mark of your privilege. It is also somehow apt.

■ ■ ■

In preferring to pray in solitude—in assuming that solitude is conducive to, even necessary for, my pursuit of intimacy with God—I am following a well-established Christian pattern. To wit, Antony's withdrawal in the desert. And even further back than that, today it is commonplace to hear pastors and spiritual directors wax eloquent about Jesus's own habit of withdrawing into a solitary space for prayer.

In the Middle Ages, men and women often joined monastic houses because, although monastic life was in many ways intensely communal, it also explicitly protected the notion of privacy, or solitude, as an integral part of the life of prayer: the monastic choreography mandated time together with other monastics, of course, but in the context of a larger monastic withdrawal from the world into solitude. In some monasteries, solitude-loving monks managed to evade some of the communal encounter ostensibly built into monastic life. When one Bishop Alnwick visited Ramsey Abbey in 1439, for example, he noted that the monks were not eating together, but were taking their meals "in several private and out of the way places," and sleeping not in the communal dormitory but "apart in separate rooms."[72]

Yet alongside the seeming solitude of prayer, praying the Daily Office places you in a community, even if you think you are praying the day's psalms alone. To pray the Daily Office is to be connected to people all around the world praying the same prayers. It is to connect yourself across time to those who have prayed these prayers before and those who will pray them after. Just as the Christian tradition has always lauded solitude, so too prayer in the Christian tradition has always been deeply communal. I think of the time some of my students have done in solitary confinement. I try to picture them praying in the hole. People who have been in solitary report that praying the hours joins them to a community of prayer. Through the Daily Office, they are isolated but praying as part of a body.

To say that praying the hours, praying the psalms, will forge bonds between you and other praying people is not just a trope, a will-of-the-wisp. Another word for those bonds is "solidarity."

72. Diana Webb, *Privacy and Solitude: The Medieval Discovery of Personal Space* (New York: Continuum, 2007), 207.

I find myself pondering the distinctions that my own brain makes and takes comfort in—distinctions between "solidarity," which I reserve for "political" contexts and "forging bonds," or "joining you to a community," or "making you part of body," which is language I use for prayer—as though prayer does not have a politics, as though "solidarity" is an alien vocabulary to, say, the prayers of Hebrew Scripture.

I am currently reading a collection of writings from the North Carolina Correctional Center for Women (NCCCW) that was published in 1976: *Break de Chains of Legalized U.$. Slavery*. The volume, which includes critiques and protests of the working conditions of and medical care available to women at the NCCCW, speaks bracingly about solidarity between those inside and those outside. Alice Wise wrote of seeing three male guards go without the required presence of a "matron" into a cell holding a female prisoner. She and several other residents of the NCCCW called for the guards to get out. As punishment for seeing what she saw, Wise was placed in an isolation unit where a male guard threatened her with a knife. "I am now in the hole with my other two sistas where we have been for forty days. Death still lurks around us. We cannot get to one another. Who then is to help us?" (It is a question that echoes the psalmist, I think: *From whence comes my help?*) "The support of all oppressed people," comes Wise's answer.[73] That is solidarity, and also the forging of bonds, the imagined creation of a community.

73. Triangle Area Lesbian Feminists, *Break de Chains of Legalized U.$. Slavery* (Raleigh, NC: Prison Book Project, 1976), 19.

A few pages later, Tarishi Maisha (Shirley Herlth) turns that solidarity explicitly to the language of psalm-prayer:

My 23rd Psalm of the Revolution!

The revolution is my life, liberation I shall all ways seek;

It maketh me stand against all injustices, and leadeth me

to educate the masses.

It strengthens my soul; it leadeth me to fight the

dehuman-ization of/for my people.

Yea; tho I walk thru the battlefield, I will fear no evil:

for my M-16 is with me; my love and devotion to the

oppressed leadeth me to strive onward.

Thou preparest the electric chair before me in the pres-

ence of

amerikkka's kapitolistis, they strap my entirity to it's

electric

currents; my life beith destroyed.

Surely the revolution shall follow me eternally, as I dwell

in the hearts of my people forever.[74]

If you follow *The Divine Hours*, you will pray Psalm 23 during a mid-November vespers, and during January at the Office of the Night Watch, and again in the fourth week of Lent, and then in May, during the Office recited at midnight. I am now praying (not always comfortably, but then I have been uncomfortable when praying an imprecatory psalm before) with Tarishi Maisha (Shirley Herlth).

74. Ibid., 64.

■ ■ ■

Since that conversation I had with Phyllis at the retreat center five years ago, I have remarried, and now there is much less time alone in my house. There is instead, a man, and his twelve-year-old daughter. I count them as gifts in many ways, of course, as abundance, as surprise, but I am also staggered by the loss— specifically the loss of solitude, the loss of time alone in my house.

Before my stepdaughter moved in, my friend Sarah told me that this would happen: "For many years," said Sarah, "your home has been the place you have retreated to, and now, like every other woman living with children, it will become the place you need to retreat from."

Recently, I told Sarah that I wished to make a thirty-day silent retreat. I was picturing an Ignatian retreat center somewhere lovely—New Orleans, or Boston, or England. I would make a seven-day silent retreat first, and over the next few years build up to a full thirty-day retreat. I was worried that I might not be able to pull it off, that I would miss Michael too much. "But I feel so in need of solitude, which I have lost," I said. I thought about Paul Mariani's book *Thirty Days*. I imagined the room in the monastery where I would spend those seven, and those thirty days, alone, mostly in silence, the simple monastic room, with a twin bed and maybe a desk. "So even though I think it will be logistically and emotionally challenging to figure out how and when to go on this retreat," I told Sarah, "I think I really need it."

Sarah stirred her coffee. She asked if I would be willing to get arrested and spend a month in solitary confinement instead.

■ ■ ■

Megan Sweeney, a scholar at the University of Michigan, has studied the practice of reading in women's prisons. What do incarcerated women read, and why? What meaning does reading take on for them? Sweeney finds that reading serves many important purposes for incarcerated women. Reading connects them to a larger world of ideas outside the prison; it gives them imaginative tools for reflecting on their pasts and considering their futures; in a place where human touch is largely forbidden and sensory pleasures are few, even the tactile and "aesthetic properties of books . . . assume . . . significance."[75]

What leapt out at me, when I read the book after teaching in a prison for a year, was Sweeney's argument that reading created a space of privacy for incarcerated women. The silence of being absorbed in a book was the only silence they could find in the prison. The privacy of reading was the only privacy they had access to. The only tranquility available to the women was the tranquility found in the experience of getting absorbed in a book. "Although having 'a room of one's own' is not possible for most [incarcerated] women," writes Sweeney, " . . . curling up in bed with a book of one's own—even if it is a borrowed book from the prison library—can provide a rare sense of peace, solitude,

---

75. Megan Sweeney, *Reading Is My Window: Books and the Art of Reading in Women's Prisons* (Chapel Hill: University of North Carolina Press, 2010), 79.

fantasy, or escape in the midst of a life governed by constant struggle and the realism of others."[76]

Over the course of the semester, our incarcerated students shared their prayers with other people. A woman might be practicing doodling prayer in the one social room, with a TV blaring. She is doodling away and another resident approaches her and wants to know what she is doing, and she teaches her friend how to doodle to God. Another woman is attending her job-training/reentry program, which meets at the Presbyterian church, and she tells the pastor, who has never walked a labyrinth, all about labyrinth prayer. And many of my students shared the practice of praying the hours with their bunkmates, because that was the person accessible to them in late evening and early morning. They weren't free to gather with other members of the class, so they prayed the hours with their bunkmates.

At the end of the semester, we devote an evening to sharing our reflections on the course with one another. One of the incarcerated women—a woman from an evangelical background who was accustomed, four months ago, to only spontaneous prayer—names the Daily Office as her favorite practice from the course. She says it is something of a relief to not be in the position of always having to generate the words of your prayers.

I wonder if there is also something for her in the implicitly corporate nature of praying the hours: how the prayers connect her to a great chain of saints who have prayed, and are praying, inside and outside prisons.

76. Ibid., 70–71.

And I wonder if the way the Offices calibrate time holds particular significance in a prison. In the introduction to *The Divine Hours*, Phyllis explains that the Roman Empire efficiently carved up the day into set hours with bells tolling to mark the time. The forum bells came to mark and count everything in the empire, including Christian prayer. I think of praying the Daily Office as overlaying "sacred" time on top of my "secular" or consumerist or capitalist time, but really the hours of the Daily Office are themselves decidedly not Christian; they are Roman hours. And the lesson I think the Daily Office holds may be precisely inverted: instead of representing the sacred's layering on top of (or reordering, or puncturing) the secular, the Daily Office may represent our ability to fit prayer in, even on someone else's calendar; we can manage to pray even if the Roman Empire is governing how we keep time. This is apposite in the prison. One of the things the state takes from incarcerated people is their capacity to order their time (we don't use the idiom *doing time* for nothing). The Daily Office may remind incarcerated women that they can pray anyway: the state may be ordering their very hours, but even inside that order they can pray.

Sarah and I are stunned when our student says that she has been praying the same week of *The Divine Hours* over and over, for the last twelve weeks. (Sarah subsequently makes arrangements for this student to have access to a breviary.)

■ ■ ■

I find myself thinking a lot about beds.

As is probably true of many people, the very first place I ever prayed was my bed: for much of my childhood, I said a pretty elaborate three-part prayer at night in bed. But I have moved on. I do not usually pray in bed anymore—I get up and go to one of my special chairs. I am reminded by the women at the prison of what radical simplicity there can be in prayer, of how little is actually required to pray. If your bed area is the only place over which you have any control (and in the prison, even that control is quite conditional, quite constrained), then the bed area becomes the place you meet God. You can pray the hours while sitting on your bed. You can move your hand around a finger labyrinth. You can imagine your way into a scriptural story. You can practice almost any form of prayer in your bed.

The prison where my students live is in some ways the opposite of prayer. Prayer is a place of freedom. The prison is a place of confinement. Prayer is a place of entering into your status as the bearer of the image of God. Prison wants to degrade and dehumanize. And yet, the longer I get to know these women, the more I realize this prison is one of the most prayer-saturated places in the state.

Remembering Megan Sweeney's analysis, I have begun to think that prayer operates a bit like reading for my students. That prayer becomes a way of exercising some control, in an institution designed precisely to take away your agency. That prayer becomes for them a space of quiet and privacy and attention-paying, in the midst of a carceral space trying to undo all of those things. That prayer becomes a space of peace in the midst of a carceral space of unpeace.

I think about how dogged my incarcerated students are, how persistent they are in finding places, times, and ways to pray. It is a chastening and emboldening witness.

Prayer is a place, indeed.

AFTERWORD

Diana Butler Bass

Mn 1998, my husband and I were invited to a dinner party in Memphis, Tennessee. When we gathered at the dining room table, our host seated me next to Phyllis Tickle. At the time, I was writing a weekly column on religion for the *New York Times* Syndicate and she was the religion editor at *Publishers Weekly*. I was also a professor at nearby Rhodes College, the same college at which Phyllis had taught years before. We were both Episcopalians. And, when she was younger, she and her husband had lived in the same neighborhood where my family now resided. Although we were separated in age by twenty-five years, we discovered that we had similar views of religion and culture, and shared the same hopes for a dynamic, renewed faith for the future. The seating arrangement was either a stroke of holy genius or a protocol flub, for Phyllis and I chatted as excitedly as teenage girls who just found their new best friend and only occasionally participated in the larger conversation.

After dinner, we lingered on the front porch, continuing the conversation there. The words of C. S. Lewis from *The Four Loves* echoed in my mind: "The typical expression of opening Friendship would be something like, 'What? You too? I thought I was the only one!'"

On a whim, I asked Phyllis if she would be a guest lecturer in the class I was teaching on Contemporary Spiritual Memoir. She smiled, her eyes sparkling, and replied, "Nothing would delight me more!"

Not long afterward, she came to my Rhodes class and held forth for almost two hours on the role of memoir in contemporary religious books (Kathleen Norris's great book, *The Cloister Walk*, was a recent bestseller), what can be learned from reading memoir, and how to approach writing one. She talked about the generational differences between baby boomers and GenX, the looming technological revolution, prayer, the pope, poetry and the liberal arts, what a vibrant church or synagogue should be like, her family, and her farm north of Memphis. A discussion *about* spiritual memoir became two hours *of* spiritual memoir, a master teacher weaving the threads of her own life, the questions of the students in the room, theology, art, and culture in a captivating narrative of God, vocation, and meaning.

As I listened, something struck me. Phyllis was sixty-four, a grandmother, and at the age when most people think of retirement. Although she was talking about memoir, there was nothing nostalgic in her tone. Instead, she spoke of a living past and a hope-filled future. What no one in that classroom fully understood at the time, perhaps not even Phyllis, was that it was not only a discussion of what had been, but it was also a preview of what would be—her next fifteen years of work.

Many things were about to change. The Internet was in its earliest stages, it was a time of books and newspapers, terrorism and a war on terror were unthinkable, the economy was in a sort of gilded age—and so was religion. Everyone thought the millennium would bring a spiritual boom, along with the unstoppable optimism of a new age. Yet, when Phyllis spoke of the future, she did not place her hope on economics, politics, or religious institutions. Instead, she conveyed passion for the past, prayer, philosophy, and prose as paths to a spiritual life with rich meaning in and for the world.

When things did collapse in the first years of the twenty-first century, Phyllis did not retire. Instead, the end of traditional publishing, the crises of Christianity, the global economic depression, the political divides, and the age of terrorism energized her. Amid the rubble of what was dying, Phyllis saw what could be born: a Great Emergence, an experiential, vibrant, ethical faith that draws from the treasures of ancient wisdom and relates to new patterns of technology and community.

Phyllis has played many parts in her life—teacher, parent, professor, author, poet, playwright, publisher, and journalist. But they all have contributed to her most significant role: prophet.

No sane person wants to be a prophet; there is no academic course of study, no job security. Prophets happen. Looking back, I wonder if that day at Rhodes College was more than a class. I wonder if we witnessed a moment of calling, the moment when Phyllis's vocational wheel turned from publishing to prophecy.

Thomas Merton once said of prophets, "There's something in your bones . . . which you must obey." He also depicted prophets as frenzied, dancing lunatics who "teach and entertain." In his poem "Advice to Young Prophets," he wrote:

America needs these fatal friends
Of God and country, to grovel in mystical ashes,
Pretty big prophets whose words don't burn,
Fighting the strenuous imago all day long.[77]

Thank you, Phyllis. You are not exactly a young prophet, rather an elder one, made all the wiser through the prism of life experience and prayer. We have needed you. You have been a "pretty big prophet." Your words will not be consumed, for they burn in the hearts of your friends forever. And we promise: we will continue the frenzied dance that you have begun toward the future.

77. Thomas Merton, *The Collected Poems of Thomas Merton* (New York: New Directions Publishing, 1980), 339.

ANNOTATED BIBLIOGRAPHY OF THE WORKS OF PHYLLIS TICKLE

Kelly Pigott

y guess is that everyone who has ever met Phyllis Tickle has a story to tell, and I am no exception. After becoming a big fan because of her *Divine Hours* series, I invited her to speak in chapel at the university where I teach. This happened to coincide with when her book *The Great Emergence* hit the shelves, so it was good timing on both sides.

I vividly remember picking her up at our small airport. I had seen pictures of a petite and glowing woman, the matriarch of a large family. So I was expecting to have an easy-going time with her. Imagine my surprise when she bolted off the plane like lightning and thundered into my world. I haven't been the same since.

All I can say is that the next twenty-four hours were a blur. When she found out I taught church history for a living, we went back and forth, with barely time enough to catch our breaths, swapping stories, laughing hysterically, and sharing conspiracy theories.

And then, right before it was time for her to get up to speak in chapel, Phyllis looked at me with an impish smile and asked, "Are you tenured?"

"What?" I said.

"Are you tenured?" she insisted.

I remember stammering as a thousand ideas came to mind, most of them involving getting fired in one fashion or another. "Um, I'm up for it next year," I answered truthfully.

"Oh, well," she said, genuinely disappointed. "I'll play it safe." And then she popped up to the pulpit.

Needless to say, she did a fantastic job, even though I didn't breathe once while she talked.

Before I said good-bye to her that afternoon, though, I discovered the side of Phyllis that I believe has endeared her to those of us who call her "friend." When she found out I was working on a manuscript, she asked to see a sample. She must have read it on the plane, for the next day I received an email. As I read it over and over that morning, I felt as if she had reached out far across the countryside and laid her hands on me with a prayer of blessing and affirmation. Her email has become a talisman that gets me through discouraging times as a writer.

And so it is with deep affection that I have put together this annotated bibliography. I wish to thank my wife, Susan, and my assistants Heidi Weik and Whitney Cloud for their help with this project. And I am especially grateful to the library staff here at Hardin-Simmons University, in particular Leta Tillman, who somehow managed to find all of these works for me to study.

1970s

■ *Figs and Fury.* Memphis, TN: St. Luke's Press, 1974.

This script is a chancel drama about the life of Jeremiah. In the introduction, Phyllis describes the genre in the following ways: it's always religious (thus designed for sacred space); it is void of props and scenery; and it promotes a hero "of truly noble proportions." The language of the script reminded me of DeMille's *Ten Commandments*, which loosely adopted a King James vocabulary and syntax to create an epic tone. Phyllis was not beyond poking a little fun at it, as she does when Jeremiah introduces himself with "I'm not yet twenty-five years old and already tired to death of pulling down altars and refusing lusty women." The narrative portrays Jeremiah as a suffering servant who foreshadows the messianic mission of Christ—a source of frustration for the prophet, but a prophecy of hope for the audience.

■ With Betty Gilow et al. *It's No Fun to Be Sick.* Memphis, TN: St. Luke's Press, 1975.

A charming book for children based on the true story of a girl named Paula. The afterword explains that Phyllis became intrigued with the project because her son John had been very sick as a child, and she remembered how scared he was. And so, she offered to help Paula write her story so that others might find comfort. The book's innocent prose is illustrated by drawings from children in a class sponsored by the Memphis Academy of Arts, where Paula was a student. The approach lent authenticity and power to the project as it was done by children for children, keeping it from becoming condescending or paternalistic.

■ With Betty Gilow. *The Story of Two Johns*. Memphis, TN: St. Luke's Press, 1976.

This children's book is based upon Phyllis's memory of her grandfather who was "never there and was always everywhere all at the same time." Betty Gilow illustrates with stunning Victorian drawings. As the story unfolds, the reader learns that as a little girl, Phyllis was very fond of her grandfather, who fought under General Lee's command at Shiloh and was severely wounded. Phyllis weaves the impressions of her grandfather that she gathers from his portrait, his house, and the stories her father told into observations about her son John. At the end of the book, she muses that though she was never able to actually see or touch her grandfather (something she cleverly hides in the story), as a young mother she has discovered that he "looks at me from young John's fine, blue eyes and makes me know that the more we live, the more there is of him." A touching tribute at the end of the book is made to her father, who died just before her son Philip was born: "unknown to one another, they have met in me."

■ *American Genesis*. Memphis, TN: St. Luke's Press, 1976.

A single poem published in honor of the nation's bicentennial about what it means to go home.

1980s

■ Editor. *On Beyond Koch*. Memphis, TN: Brooks Memorial Art Gallery, 1981.

A work about teaching poetry to children, written in honor of Kenneth Koch. Poetry written by children from Memphis elementary schools provides the bulk of the work. Phyllis writes an informative introduction that in itself makes the book a worthy text for elementary English teachers. But for noneducators, there are beautiful poems to read and share with children to inspire them to do the same. Two chapters describe a couple of afternoon sessions where educators introduced the craft of writing poetry to children. The appendices provide cited poems, including those written by Phyllis. Also in the appendices is a history of the Brooks program in Memphis, which was the basis for the book. Finally, the work includes an annotated bibliography for those seeking further study into the world of teaching poetry to children—a little dated but still quite useful.

▪ Editor, with Vangie Piper. *On Beyond AIS*. Memphis, TN: Raccoon Books, Inc., 1982.

This collection of essays is a companion volume to *On Beyond Koch*. In it, the editors evaluate the Artists in the Schools (AIS) program in Tennessee, with a look at where the program might grow in the future. It is divided into four sections. "AIS Goes to Town" discusses cultural changes around Tennessee. "AIS in a Gown" delves into the mechanics of introducing students to the arts. In this section, Phyllis provides an essay entitled "Frocking AIS," where she argues that the practice of teaching the arts to students isn't necessarily to make them artists, but rather "that they may gain the tools of perception, of insightful and personal contact with absolute and immutable reality. . . . We train, not for art, but for wholeness." The next section, "AIS Under the Looking Glass" is a utilitarian look at pedagogy. Finally, "AIS and . . . " provides a look at the AIS program within the Tennessee context.

■ *Tobias and the Angels*. Memphis, TN: St. Luke's Press, 1982.
This is a script for a drama based on the apocryphal
book Tobit. A similar work was also published under the
title *Puppeteers for Our Lady,* as a narrated mime show.
The former provides an informative introduction for the
ancient work, summarizing the narrative and providing
brief literary criticism. Once again, Phyllis shows off her
wit with engaging dialogue while tackling heady questions
of theodicy and existentialism. At one point she has the
main character, Tobias, ask of the angel Raphael, "If our
bodies and our souls never connect, the creation is just
an amusement park for God and we're all just puppets.
And you become some kind of master puppeteer for
his entertainment." Tension builds between the two until
toward the end of the play Tobias yells in frustration, "I still
want the explanation! The why of all this charade! Some
spiritual justification beyond divine amusement for all this
physical pain and death." One cannot only hear the cries
of an ancient Near-Eastern writer facing a cruel world, but
also the voice of a modern young mother who suffered a
series of miscarriages in rural Tennessee.

■ *The City Essays*. Memphis, TN: Dixie Flyer's Press, 1982.
This brief, fifty-page book is a collection of essays
contrasting city and country life. In the foreword, Phyllis
confesses that as one who has lived in both locales, the
two "differ from each other very little." She was prompted
to write these essays during the latter 1970s and early
1980s as a response to her "fascination with the city both
as a political entity and as a divine concept." Subjects
vary from personal experiences—like the time she was
accosted in a grocery store—to the historical, where she
muses on the likes of Nero and Anne Hutchinson. This
collection is a good example of Phyllis's keen observation

skills and her introspection, coupled with her obsession with history. The musings are as much about comparing geographical cultures as they are about showing how the modern world has been shaped by history. And in this, one sees the first inklings of the thesis that will dominate her later writings.

▪ *Selections*. **Notre Dame, IN: Erasmus Books of Notre Dame, 1983.** A small, wonderful collection of Phyllis's poems, several of which were previously published. They are organized into four sections. "The Lucy Poems" represent those written about life at the farm in Lucy. Many of these were inspired by holy days like Michaelmas, All Saints, and Easter. "Burglary" is a dark poem about someone who broke into her house and stole cherished heirlooms while she was away.

> Someday I will shoot you
> Between the bedrooms and the kitchen door;
> Or I will write a poem
> That leaves you bleeding there.

"Selections from the GE Poems" contains poems mainly about significant people and events in her life. They include "Miscarriage" where she pens,

> My unfilled hours settle into days
> and grief wearies into sadness.

"The Anniversary Song" is a tender tribute to her marriage to Sam, where the refrain "you in your knickers and I in my gown" echoes through memories. And "Interstate 40" playfully begins,

> The autumn vinegar
> Of a startled skunk
> Roughs my nose

The third section, "The Natalie Bartlum Poems," are
a collaborative effort between Phyllis and Margaret
Bartlum Ingraham. And the last section is a single poem,
"American Genesis," previously published.

▪ With Dennie L. Smith and Lana J. Smith. *Seeing Through Stone:
A Teacher's Guide to Lessons in Poetry.* Memphis, TN: Memphis
Brooks Museum, 1984.

This text was written by Dennie L. Smith and Lana J.
Smith, based on Phyllis's work as the poet-in-residence at
the Memphis Brooks Museum. It was a project sponsored
by the Memphis Brooks Museum and the Tennessee
Arts Commission. Consisting of eleven lessons, the book
targets teachers who may or may not have experience in
poetry, and it provides them with a resource that can be
used "for teaching about and [for the] writing of quality
poetry." Phyllis describes the work as an instruction in
"studio poetry" in contrast to a class about poetry. She
continues, "[W]e are not teaching about the result of craft,
but we are, instead, teaching the rudiments of the craft
in order that the student may arrive at the emotional and
intuitive information and patterns of perception which
are the vitality and integrity of the art itself." No doubt,
the work came from the stars and scars Phyllis earned
while attempting to teach young students how to be
wordsmiths.

▪ *The Tickle Papers.* Nashville, TN: Abingdon Press, 1989.

This is a collection of autobiographical stories pondering
the meaning of vocation. Previously published as a
trilogy by Upper Room Books, the essays are organized
around the liturgical year. I comment on this trilogy later

when it comes to full fruition in the Stories from the
Farm in Lucy series. But suffice it to say that when *The
Tickle Papers* was printed, Phyllis had already established
herself in this genre, even though this is the first time
such a book is annotated. And by now she has polished
her craft. Phyllis's keen sense of observation and poetic
voice create a delightful work that invites the reader
into a game, to use Phyllis's own metaphor, a game
primarily played with children. The seventeen chapters
are organized into three sections: "Called to This Life,"
"Concrete Abstractions," and "The Sign of the Eagle." In
"Called to This Life," Phyllis's daughter Laura takes her to
task after school one day for having so many siblings.
Laura chides, "If you just wouldn't chase Daddy all over
the place all the time, it wouldn't happen." Bemused,
Phyllis tries to defend herself, but to no avail. At the end
of the day, Laura spies her parents and cries, "See, you're
doing it again." Phyllis explains to Sam, "She thinks I
should quit chasing you." In response the father declares
to Laura, "Wrong. . . . Your mother was called to this life."
And with that, Sam knocks the ball out of the park, over
the heads of both mother and daughter. And the game's
afoot.

1990s

■ Editor. *Confessing Conscience: Churched Women on Abortion.*
Nashville, TN: Abingdon Press, 1990.

In this collection of raw essays, Phyllis invited eleven
women from various backgrounds and denominations
to share their views and experiences within the abortion
debate. They include Marilou Awiakta, Sarai Schnucker

Beck, Colleen C. Conant, Judith Craig, Roberta Kells
Dorr, Judy Mathe Foley, Jo Kicklighter, Lurlene McDaniel,
Sandra O. Smithson, Martha Ellen Stortz, and Juli Loesch
Wiley. In part, this is a reaction to the politicization of the
issue that so easily dichotomizes the subject into extreme
camps. Each essayist was asked to express her view on
the debate and then to wrestle with the question, "What
now of your Christianity?" The views are as unique as the
individuals who wrote them. And yet they are unified in
their femininity. "All of us have bled and it is the power
and the ancient magic of that dark flow that we come,
hoping to further the healing of the nation." Phyllis begins
the collection, sharing her connection to the issue as
experienced through her many miscarriages. Each child
lost was "like Banquo's ghost, as tangible and informative
as any idea appertained." Her concluding essay links the
abortion debate for women with the Vietnam debate
for men. For both genders, the politics of life and death,
freedom and justice must be governed with wisdom and
peace.

▪ *My Father's Prayer.* Nashville, TN: Upper Room Books, 1995.
This small jewel is a book of poetic prose describing
Phyllis's experience as a very young girl at home during
World War II. She chose poignant moments to write
about, beginning with a phone call informing the family
of a deceased uncle. And then the narrative moves to
the exact moment when her father realized that war was
inevitable. "He was too old to go, too young to watch.
In the place of both, he wept." Soon after, she discovers
him crocheting a rosette coverlet. A bit shocked that such

a masculine figure would endeavor to work on such a feminine craft, she innocently asked, "Does Mama know you're doing it?" prompting a smile from her father. The coverlet then becomes the metaphor for her "father's prayer" during the war. It was a project he continued to work on until the very end of the war. She concludes, "This book is about a space interior to us all and about how he taught me to go there." For "when hands and thoughts are occupied in the goodness of small and needful creation, the spirit rests that deep rest in which it can attend itself and be attended by the sacred." The book was republished in 2003 (after the war on terror was declared) by Paraclete Press under the title *A Stitch and a Prayer*. In this edition, Phyllis added, "While this is the story of my father, [it] is also the myth of my father."

■ *Re-Discovering the Sacred: Spirituality in America.* New York: Crossroad Publishing Company, 1995.

This is the first work where Phyllis begins to seriously delve into the question "What's next for the church?" *Re-Discovering the Sacred* starts with the observation that Americans are devouring religious books, though not necessarily Christian ones. This leads Phyllis to wonder if the spike in fascination for all things spiritual is leading somewhere. The rest of the book is a journey to connect this phenomenon with other cultural milestones like Hiroshima, Vietnam, and the "lost frontier" in the hopes of seeing what kind of picture might take shape. Using her own metaphor, Phyllis attempts to track the money and time spent on the spiritual obsessions of American culture to create a contour map of things to come. Critics charged her with arbitrarily seeing patterns where none existed. Nonetheless, the work managed to expose a cultural shift that played a significant role in popularizing a conversation about whether or not we are in the midst of a new religious paradigm, a theme that will become Phyllis's passion.

▪ **Editor, with Alice Swanson.** *HomeWorks: A Book of Tennessee Writers.* **Knoxville, TN: University of Tennessee Press, 1996.**

This anthology highlights Tennessee writers as a companion volume to the previously published *HomeWords* (University of Tennessee Press), a brainchild of Douglas Paschall. It is jointly sponsored by the University of Tennessee and the Tennessee Arts Commission. It highlights poets, fiction writers, and essayists as a part of Tennessee's bicentennial, and it is loosely organized by the ages of the contributors. Phyllis describes the work as codified by an attitude of "raw-boned grace and credible expectations." The editors chose the title because they view the collection as one of "heart and mind, done from and for home."

▪ *God-Talk in America.* **New York: Crossroad Publishing Company, 1998.**

Phyllis continues to probe the juxtaposition of theology and culture in this stream-of-consciousness-style work that she describes as a dance. As the title suggests, the book begins with the observation that Americans seem to be obsessed with talking about God. Continuing her thesis from *Re-Discovering the Sacred*, she points out that we are not only voraciously reading about God in books, but also that theology is everywhere: sitcoms, movies, beauty shops, music, and the dinner table. She suggests that a democratization of theology is taking place, which has moved the conversation from seminaries and theological schools to the marketplace. This isn't anything new. In the fourth century, Gregory of Nyssa once famously complained, "If in this city you ask anyone for change, he will discuss with you whether the Son is begotten or unbegotten." Phyllis would respond to this by pointing out that in a postmodern era there is no ecumenical council (or magisterium or episcopacy or any institution) providing accountability. Drawing from the likes of Joseph Campbell, Bill Moyers, Carl Jung, even Della Reese (from the TV show *Touched by an Angel*), Phyllis infers that our God-talk arises "more from an acceleration of experience than from any actual spiritual stupidity on our part as a people." And in her estimation, this is a good thing. Copious endnotes are provided.

2000s

The Divine Hours Series

Phyllis reaches back and resurrects the ancient practice formalized by St. Benedict of praying the hours, also known as the Daily Offices. It's not the first work to update and modify this practice for the laity, but it will certainly remain a classic for some time. Phyllis draws from sources such as the Book of Common Prayer, the early church fathers, hymns, poetry and texts mainly from the Jerusalem Bible to provide a morning, noon, and evening discipline of prayer. A separate section provides the monthly compline for bedtime. The collection modifies and contemporizes the archaic and breathes fresh air into an ancient practice that has become quite popular among those who have felt drawn to the ancient forms of prayer and worship.

■ *The Divine Hours: Prayers for Summertime.* New York: Doubleday, 2000.

The first of the series to be published, it begins in June during "Ordinary Time" in the liturgical calendar and includes some of the major feasts for this period. It concludes with September.

■ *The Divine Hours: Prayers for Autumn and Wintertime.* New York: Doubleday, 2000.

This volume begins in October and includes Advent, Christmas, and Epiphany, along with the corresponding major feasts. It concludes with January.

■ *The Divine Hours: Prayers for Springtime.* New York: Doubleday, 2001.

This volume begins in February and includes Lent, Easter, Ascensiontide, and Pentecost along with the corresponding major feasts. It concludes with May.

■ *Christmastide: Prayers for Advent through Epiphany.* New York: Doubleday, 2003.

As the title suggests, this volume concentrates on the time frame from Advent through Epiphany.

▪ *The Shaping of a Life: A Spiritual Landscape.* New York: Image Books/Doubleday, 2003.

In the grand tradition of Augustine's *Confessions*, *The Shaping of a Life* is an autobiography describing Phyllis's gradual awakening to matters of the spirit. After a brief stay in her childhood, the narrative lingers in her young-adult years as she attends Shorter College in Georgia. Later, she marries Sam, who becomes a county doctor; the two raise a family, and she ventures into education, writing, and publishing. In the first sentence Phyllis declares, "My father taught me to love words, and my mother taught me to pray." Words and prayer then become a common theme as she discovers not only St. Benedict's discipline of the hours, but also the truth behind his axiom, "To pray is to work and to work is to pray." In this respect, she discovers that the Spirit is found as readily in a hymn or a T. S. Eliot poem as he is in the rearing of children, the travails of marriage, and in the suffrage of insufferable preaching. She concludes, "In caterpillars and babies, introspective writers find the most obvious examples of the patterns and mystery that we all perceive to be the stuff, as well as the story, of our selves."

Stories from The Farm in Lucy Series

This three-volume series is self-described as "a collection of facts that have been owned down into stories." In the prologue, Phyllis describes the epiphany she and her husband, Sam, had in 1976 that their children "possessed none of the freedom or the discipline that come from knowing how to live with and on the land." As a result, they bought what became known as "The Farm in Lucy" just outside Memphis, Tennessee. She draws upon the resulting experiences with her family and the land and weaves them into the liturgical year in a collection of witty and clever essays. They are based on the premise, "Religion has always kept earth time. Liturgy only gives sanction to what the heart already knows." This series is a revision of an earlier trilogy published by Upper Room Books in Nashville.

■ *What the Land Already Knows: Winter's Sacred Days.* Chicago: Loyola Press, 2003.

Phyllis begins the series appropriately with eleven essays on the beginning of the liturgical year, including Advent, Christmas, and Epiphany, with little-known celebrations like the feast of Stephen thrown in. Authors typically think long and hard about how to begin a book because they know it not only has to capture the attention of the audience, but it also must set the tone for the rest of the work. And Phyllis handles this masterfully in her very first story, "The Vining Wreath." In it, she describes a wonderful scene where Sam cares for an arbor around the patio where he grew large, plump grapes. You can almost feel her blush when she describes how his work made her think "about his hands, a lover's hands among the vines." This work is a revision of an earlier title, *What the Heart Already Knows* (Nashville: Upper Room Books, 1985).

■ *Wisdom in the Waiting: Spring's Sacred Days.* Chicago: Loyola Press, 2004.

The book continues the series with fourteen essays on the sacred days of spring, including Fat Tuesday,

Lent, Holy Week, Easter, and Pentecost. The previously published essay "Final Sanity" won the Polly Bond Award. The book describes Lent as "the greatest calm in the church's year" before summer's "too much color, too much noise, too much growing." In one notable essay, "Runaway Son," she taps into the fear of every parent as she describes her frantic search for her five-year-old son Sam, Jr. After a chilling description of a neighbor poking at the bottom of the pond with a pitchfork, the story ends happily. And Phyllis reveals the lesson she learned about how one must move "from nightmares into faith." This work is a revision of an earlier title, *Final Sanity* (Nashville: Upper Room Books, 1987).

▪ *The Graces We Remember: Sacred Days of Ordinary Time.* Chicago: Loyola Press, 2004.

The final book of the series includes twelve essays about the liturgical calendar after Pentecost. Phyllis bemoans how "ordinary" is used to describe half the liturgical year, a description "stark in its simplicity, for, as we all know, there is no such thing." Case in point, she connects the Feast of the Transfiguration with a facetious story that a ghost named Lawrence lives in her house. She concludes, "He has given me the liberating proof that I am out of my depth, that I am inconsistent, that I don't know how to use things that I both see and sometimes don't see." This work is a revision of an earlier title, *Ordinary Time: Stories of the Days between Ascensiontide and Advent* (Nashville: Upper Room Books, 1988).

■ *Greed: The Seven Deadly Sins,* New York: Oxford University Press, 2004.

Elda Rotor is the editor of this seven-book series sponsored by Oxford University Press and the New York Public Library. In an interview, Phyllis confessed she had first asked for "lust," but the editor discouraged her, pointing out that the matriarch of a large family may not be the most credible voice for that particular subject. So she chose greed, which she concludes is the prime sin leading to all others. She points to such texts as "the love of money is the root of all evil." In this brief book she utilizes works of art as talking points, like Pieter Breugel's "Big Fish Little Fish" where in the stomach of a very large fish are smaller fish who have in their stomachs yet smaller fish to illustrate where greed leads. In addition, she reflects on Hieronymous Bosch's "The Haywain" where people are trampled by a hay cart as they reach for the treasures inside. She concludes with Mario Donizetti's "Avarice," and points out (prayerfully, perhaps) that we live in a time when moderns see more clearly that greed has "begun to shrink into herself."

■ *Prayer Is a Place: America's Religious Landscape Observed.* New York: Doubleday, 2005.

Once again, Phyllis attempts to describe the paradigm shift in the religious landscape from the inside-out. This time she weaves her observations into a narrative from her days of working in the publishing industry when spiritual books went from a few shelves in the dark corners of bookstores to row upon row prominently displayed front and center. She proffers that the years 1992–2004 were "a reconfiguration and cultural repositioning that history will, I wager, see as having been more comparable to the upheavals of Europe during the Christian Reformation." Time will tell whether or not this is hyperbole. Nevertheless, she expresses gratitude that she was lucky enough to be "standing on the street corner, pad and pencil in hand. . . . as the parade went by." This work represents what she wrote down on that pad.

■ *This Is What I Pray Today: The Divine Hours Prayers for Children.* New York: Dutton Children's Books (a division of Penguin Young Readers Group), 2007.

Beautifully illustrated by Elsa Warnick, this work introduces very young children to the discipline of fixed-hour prayer. Beginning with a poem that starts, "Three times each day, Little children like to pray," the book follows up with three prayers for each day of the week under the headings "Waking Up," "Resting," and "Ending My Day."

■ *The Words of Jesus: A Gospel of the Sayings of Our Lord with Reflections by Phyllis Tickle.* San Francisco: Wiley/Jossey-Bass, 2008.

During lunch with a colleague, Phyllis was asked if she had ever pondered what it would be like to strip the Gospels down to just the words of Jesus. Recognizing that every editor and author has an agenda, it makes sense that the Gospel writers perhaps made subtle changes in order to make Jesus's words a little more palatable. Stripped of this, what would the Gospels reveal? In an interview, she answered, "This is not the meek and mild Jesus that many of us are comfortable with. He is bold and radical and it's clear to see why so many followed Him and why so many others wanted Him

dead." At one point Jesus says to "love your enemies," and
then says He came "to bring the sword and division." At
another, he dismisses Mary, asking, "Who is my mother?"
And then on the cross he says tenderly, "Woman, behold
your son." Why the differences? Phyllis says, "Once was
the time I would have regarded such a discovery as
close to irreverent and a threat to His godness. Now I
embrace it with a kind of fond gratitude." The book is
organized into five categories: public teaching, private
instruction, healing dialogue, intimate conversation,
and postresurrection encounters. It includes a fifty-page
introductory commentary.

■ *The Great Emergence: How Christianity Is Changing and Why.*
Grand Rapids, MI: Baker Books, 2008.

Arguably Phyllis's *magnum opus*, *The Great Emergence*
represents the pinnacle of her thoughts on the paradigm
shift happening as postmodernity slams into Christianity.
The title is a little deceptive. This is not a book just about
the emerging church movement, but the worldwide
paradigm shift happening to Christianity, of which the
emerging church movement in the United States is a part.
Phyllis's thesis (which she admits getting from the Right
Reverend Mark Dryer) is that every 500 years the church
goes through a major paradigm shift. She identifies
them as The Great Decline and Fall, The Great Schism,
The Great Reformation, and now the Great Emergence.
Each 500-year epoch roughly follows a similar pattern,
beginning with a rummage sale where the institutional
church is forced to get rid of baggage that has made
it irrelevant to the current generation. Out of the ashes

of this upheaval comes a new and reinvigorated form of Christianity. The old form still exists, but leaner and more pure. The pattern concludes with an expansion of the faith into a new part of the world and to a new demographic group. Phyllis further argues that we are currently in such a paradigm shift characterized by, among other things, a more Jewish (rather than Hellenistic) theology; an emphasis on community; a demotion of orthodoxy over the primacy of orthopraxy; and a struggle for what will become the new authority to replace the Reformation doctrine of *sola scriptura*. The jury is still out on the lattermost, but the wrestling ring includes such characters as pneumatology, "orthonomy," "theonomy" (the grand narrative), and crowd-sourcing, all of which she defines for the sake of the reader.

The book sparked a lively conversation. Barbara Newman, former president of the prestigious Church History Society, wrote on its website, "Cherry-picking dates from church history cannot prove, by some Marxian iron law, that we now stand at an epoch-making turn." And on the other end of the spectrum, author Diana Butler Bass offered on the book jacket, "After reading these pages, neither the church nor the world looks the same." Regardless, one cannot argue with the fact that from universities and seminaries to churches and coffee houses, this book prompted people to ponder whether or not we are living in a moment that will dramatically change the course of the Jesus movement that began two millennia ago.

■ General Editor. The Ancient Practices series. Nashville: Thomas Nelson.

Phyllis oversees this project that entails seven volumes. As a corollary to her thesis that the church is going through a paradigm shift, she suggests that with something new comes something old—namely, that believers hunger for the mystery, discipline, and sacrifice of ancient practices. The works include *Finding Our Way Again*, by Brian McLaren (2008); *In Constant Prayer*, by Robert Benson (2009); *Sabbath*, by Dan B. Allender (2009); *Fasting*, by Scot McKnight (2009); *The Sacred Meal*, by Nora Gallagher (2009); *The Pilgrimage*, by Diana Butler Bass (2009); *The Liturgical Year*, by Joan Chittister (2010); and *Tithing*, by Douglas LeBlanc (2010). For each work, Phyllis provides a foreword, introducing the author and providing context for how the work fits into the overall series.

2010s

■ With Tim Scorer. *Embracing Emergence Christianity*. New York: Morehouse Publishing, 2011.

This is a workbook and DVD based on *The Great Emergence*. This work is part of an overall collection entitled the Embracing Series produced by a publishing arm of the Episcopal Church. Designed for small groups, Phyllis interacts with a group of people in six sessions: (1) Emergence 101, (2) Where Now Is the Authority? (3) The 20th Century and Emergence, (4) Gifts from Other Times, (5) How Then Shall We Live? and (6) Hallmarks of Emergence.

▪ *Emergence Christianity: What It Is, Where It Is Going, and Why It Matters.* Grand Rapids, MI: Baker Books, 2012.

This is the second installment of Phyllis's observations about the changes happening to Christianity in a postmodern, post-Christian world. It's broken into four parts: (1) telling the story so far, (2) how did we get here? (3) defining what it is and what it is not, and (4) thoughts on the decisions and dilemmas to come. A photographic report is also included.

Within the twenty-two chapters, one finds a dizzying summary of the many leaders and movements commanding the stage of worldwide Christianity. Phyllis weaves their stories into the grand narrative she sees happening in emergence Christianity in an attempt to give the movement some form. The end of the book provides some analysis, and perhaps a little prophecy, about where all of this is headed. She elucidates on themes addressed in her previous works pertaining to authority, community, doctrine (highlighting atonement), and polity. She concludes that she is becoming even more convinced of the importance of emergence Christianity (if that was ever in doubt), defining it in its simplest form as "a human conversation among human conversants." She ponders "what has happened in our lifetime seems to be more than just another semi-millennial shift. It seems instead to be more akin to the Great Transformation of two-thousand years ago: less a fifth turning than a great and monumental shift."

■ With Jon M. Sweeney. *The Age of the Spirit: How the Ghost of An Ancient Controversy Is Shaping the Church.* Grand Rapids, MI: Baker Books, 2014.

This is the third installment in Phyllis's reflections on emergence, and a collaboration that provides an engaging history of pneumatology, beginning with the *filioque* controversy that led to the Great Schism of 1054. One might call it a "People's History of the Holy Spirit." Written for laypeople, the authors provide a much-needed context for the current fascination with the Holy Spirit, offering some insight as to why we are still wrestling with the nature and role of this enigmatic person of the Trinity.

ABOUT THE CONTRIBUTORS

TONY JONES (tonyj.net) is the theologian-in-residence at Solomon's Porch in Minneapolis. He's the author of a dozen books, including *The New Christians: Dispatches from the Emergent Frontier, The Teaching of the Twelve,* and *The Church Is Flat: The Relational Ecclesiology of the Emerging Church Movement.* Tony teaches at several universities and seminaries, including Fuller Theological Seminary and United Theological Seminary, where he is distinguished lecturer in the practice of theology. He blogs daily at Theoblogy. He lives in Minnesota with his wife, Courtney, and three children.

JON M. SWEENEY is an independent scholar, author, and culture critic with a wide range of interests. He is the author of twenty books, including the popular *The Pope Who Quit: A True Medieval Tale of Mystery, Death, and Salvation,* published in 2012 by Image/Random House, which became a History Book Club selection and was optioned by HBO. Jon has worked in book publishing for a quarter century. For many years, he was the vice president of marketing for Jewish Lights Publishing in Vermont, as well as the cofounder and editor-in-chief of SkyLight Paths Publishing. Since 2004, he has been the editor-in-chief, and now publisher, of Paraclete Press in Massachusetts. He is married, the father of three, and lives in Ann Arbor, Michigan.

JANA RIESS is the author or coauthor of many books, including *Flunking Sainthood: A Year of Breaking the Sabbath, Forgetting to Pray, and Still Loving My Neighbor,* and *The Twible: All the Chapters of the Bible in 140 Characters or Less . . . Now with 68% More Humor!* She blogs about Mormonism and culture for Religion News Service and holds degrees in religion from Wellesley College, Princeton Theological Seminary, and Columbia University. She has worked in the publishing industry since 1999 with positions at *Publishers Weekly,* Westminster John Knox Press, and Patheos.

DANIELLE DWYER is a religious sister at the Community of Jesus and has been a member there since 1982. She has worked in many arms of ministry at the community, including cooking, finances, and hospitality, but her main focus has been the arts, especially theater. A founding member of Elements Theatre Company, Sr. Danielle has either directed or performed in nearly sixty productions since the company's inception in 1992. Classically trained but also skilled in contemporary drama, Sr. Danielle earned her master of arts degree from England's Royal Academy of Dramatic Art and the University of London. She is the author of several performance pieces, including short stories and plays, video scripts, poetic monologues, and narratives for worship and meditation.

STEPHANIE SPELLERS is the author of *Radical Welcome: Embracing the God, the Other and the Spirit of Transformation* and serves as canon for missional vitality in the diocese of Long Island, where she stirs up the 146 Episcopal churches in Brooklyn, Queens, and Long Island. Founding priest for The Crossing community at St. Paul's Episcopal Cathedral in Boston, she is the chaplain to the Episcopal House of Bishops and recent chair for the church's Standing Commission on Mission and Evangelism. Stephanie gathers and reflects on missional resources at www. missionalvitality.org.

RYAN K. BOLGER joined the Fuller Theological Seminary faculty in 2002 and is associate professor of church in contemporary culture in the School of Intercultural Studies. With his research focusing on the emerging and missional church movements, he teaches classes on contemporary culture, including postmodern and new media cultures, exploring the implications of these cultures for Christian witness. With Eddie Gibbs, he wrote *Emerging Churches.*

BRIAN D. MCLAREN is a speaker and writer whose books include *A New Kind of Christian, A Generous Orthodoxy,* and *Why Did Jesus, Moses, the Buddha, and Mohammed Cross the Road?* He began his career as a college English teacher and then served as a church-planter and pastor for over twenty years in the Washington, DC, area. He and his wife, Grace, live in Florida. They have four adult children and four grandchildren. Brian blogs at www.brianmclaren.net.

SYBIL MACBETH is a dancer, a doodler, and a former community college mathematics professor. She now combines her experience in the mathematics classroom with her lifelong love of prayer to offer workshops and retreats that engage differing learning styles. She is the author of *Praying in Color: Drawing a New Path to God*, *Praying in Color: Kids' Edition*, *Praying in Black and White: A Hands-On Practice for Men* (a collaboration with her Episcopal priest husband Andy MacBeth), and *Praying in Color: The Portable Edition*. *Praying in Color* has been translated into Korean, Spanish, and Italian.

DOUG PAGITT is a pastor, author, business owner, speaker, consultant, and radio show host. He seeks to be a social and theological entrepreneur and goodness conspirator. Doug is married to Shelley; they live in Minneapolis, Minnesota, and are parents of four young-adult children. He is the founding pastor of Solomon's Porch, a holistic, missional Christian community in Minneapolis, Minnesota, and he has written many books on church and life, including the Inventive Age Series.

LAUREN F. WINNER is the author of *Girl Meets God*, *Mudhouse Sabbath*, and *Still*. An Episcopal priest, she lives in Durham, North Carolina, where she teaches at Duke University Divinity School.

DIANA BUTLER BASS is an author, speaker, and independent scholar specializing in American religion and culture. Her books include *Christianity After Religion: The End of Church and the Birth of a New Spiritual Awakening* and *Christianity for the Rest of Us: How the Neighborhood Church Is Transforming the Faith*. She and her family live in Alexandria, Virginia.

KELLY PIGOTT is an associate professor of church history at Hardin-Simmons University, where he teaches in the Logsdon School of Theology and Logsdon Seminary and serves as the university chaplain. He's written for several academic journals and serves on the editorial board for two Baptist history societies. He loves Cajun cooking, jazz, hiking, camping, roasting his own coffee, warm conversations with his friends, silence, solitude, and words. He is especially passionate about his family—his wife, Susan, and children Nathaniel and Eliana. He blogs at kellypigott .com.

ABOUT PARACLETE PRESS

Who We Are

Paraclete Press is a publisher of books, recordings, and DVDs on Christian spirituality. Our publishing represents a full expression of Christian belief and practice—from Catholic to Evangelical, from Protestant to Orthodox.

We are the publishing arm of the Community of Jesus, an ecumenical monastic community in the Benedictine tradition. As such, we are uniquely positioned in the marketplace without connection to a large corporation and with informal relationships to many branches and denominations of faith.

What We Are Doing

Books Paraclete publishes books that show the richness and depth of what it means to be Christian. Although Benedictine spirituality is at the heart of all that we do, we publish books that reflect the Christian experience across many cultures, time periods, and houses of worship. We publish books that nourish the vibrant life of the church and its people—books about spiritual practice, formation, history, ideas, and customs.

We have several different series, including the best-selling Paraclete Essentials and Paraclete Giants series of classic texts in contemporary English; Voices from the Monastery—men and women monastics writing about living a spiritual life today; award-winning poetry; best-selling gift books for children on the occasions of baptism and first communion; and the Active Prayer Series that brings creativity and liveliness to any life of prayer.

Recordings From Gregorian chant to contemporary American choral works, our music recordings celebrate sacred choral music through the centuries. Paraclete distributes the recordings of the internationally acclaimed choir Gloriæ Dei Cantores, praised for their "rapt and fathomless spiritual intensity" by *American Record Guide,* and the Gloriæ Dei Cantores Schola, which specializes in the study and performance of Gregorian chant. Paraclete is also the exclusive North American distributor of the recordings of the Monastic Choir of St. Peter's Abbey in Solesmes, France, long considered to be a leading authority on Gregorian chant.

Videos Our videos offer spiritual help, healing, and biblical guidance for life issues: grief and loss, marriage, forgiveness, anger management, facing death, and spiritual formation.

Learn more about us at our website:
www.paracletepress.com
or call us toll-free at 1-800-451-5006.

SCAN
TO
READ
MORE

THE INTENTIONAL CHRISTIAN COMMUNITY HANDBOOK

DAVID JANZEN

Foreword by Shane Claiborne and Jonathan Wilson-Hartgrove

In the twenty-first century, a new generation of Spirit-energized people is searching for a new—yet ancient—way of life together. David Janzen, a friend of the New Monasticism movement with four decades of personal communal experience, has visited scores of communities, both old and new. This book shares his wisdom, as well as the experience of intentional Christian communities across North America over the last half century.

ISBN: 978-1-61261-237-9 • PAPERBACK • $19.99

YOU MAY ALSO BE INTERESTED IN ...

DRAWN IN

TROY BRONSINK

By understanding God in this creative way, all Christians are invited to be "drawn in" to the creative, ongoing, divine work. Exercises invite participation in God's life and redemptive rhythms and opens to church leaders a new way of thinking of mission, worship, collaboration, and everyday discipleship.

ISBN: 978-1-55725-871-7 • PAPERBACK • $16.99

THE TEACHING OF THE TWELVE

TONY JONES

The Didache is an early handbook of an anonymous Christian community spelling out a way of life for Jesus-followers, how to love one another, how to practice the Eucharist, and how to take in wandering prophets.

ISBN: 978-1-55725-590-7 • PAPERBACK • $14.99